Pronunciation Guide

VOWEL SOUNDS

Symbol	Examples
a	**a**ct, b**a**t
ā	d**a**y, **a**ge
âr	**air**, d**are**
ä	f**a**ther, st**ar**
e	**e**dge, t**e**n
ē	sp**ee**d, mon**ey**
ə*	**a**go, syst**e**m, eas**i**ly, **c**ompete, foc**u**s
ər	butt**er**, p**er**cent
ēr	d**ear**, p**ier**
i	f**i**t, **i**s
ī	sk**y**, b**i**te
o	n**o**t, w**a**sp
ō	n**o**se, **o**ver
ô	l**aw**, f**ough**t
ôr	**or**der, m**ore**
oi	n**oi**se, enj**oy**
ōō	tr**ue**, b**oo**t
oo	p**u**t, l**oo**k
yōō	c**u**te, **u**nited
ou	l**ou**d, c**ow**
u	f**u**n, **u**p
ûr	l**ear**n, **ur**ge, f**ir**m, w**or**d

* This symbol, the *schwa*, represents the sound of unaccented vowels. It sounds like "uh." Refer to the next page for more information on pronunciation matters.

CONSONANT SOUNDS

Symbol	Examples
b	**b**ack, ca**b**
ch	**ch**eap, ma**tch**, pic**t**ure
d	**d**oor, hea**d**
f	**f**an, lea**f**, **ph**one
g	**g**ive, do**g**
h	**h**er, be**h**ave
j	**j**ust, pa**g**e
k	**k**ing, ba**k**e, **c**ar
l	**l**eaf, ro**ll**
m	**m**y, ho**m**e
n	**n**ote, rai**n**
ng	si**ng**, ba**n**k
p	**p**ut, sto**p**
r	**r**ed, fa**r**
s	**s**ay, pa**ss**
sh	**sh**ip, pu**sh**
t	**t**o, le**t**
th	**th**in, wi**th**
TH	**th**at, ba**th**e
v	**v**alue, li**v**e
w	**w**ant, a**w**ay
y	**y**es, on**i**on
z	**z**oo, ma**z**e, ri**s**e
zh	plea**s**ure, vi**s**ion

Pronunciation Matters

Learning how to pronounce words will make you more likely to use the words you learn. Sometimes you may even know a word by sound and not recognize the way it is spelled; after you sound out the word, you may realize that you know it. The pronunciation guide on the previous page will help you sound out the words in this text. The pronunciations are given in the Word List for each chapter.

The symbols used here are found in several dictionaries. There are slight differences in pronunciation symbols used in dictionaries, but a pronunciation guide is usually found in the front of a dictionary and at the bottom of each page. If you are unsure of how to pronounce a word, ask your instructor or another knowledgeable person to say the word for you.

Accent Marks and Stress

An important skill in pronouncing words is learning how to decipher accent marks. The primary accent mark (′) is a dark mark. Any word that has more than one syllable will have a primary accent mark. This mark tells you which syllable to add stress to when you pronounce it. For example, in the word *replace* [ri plās′], more emphasis is put on the second syllable, as illustrated by the primary accent mark.

In words that have more than two syllables, there is sometimes a secondary accent mark (′). This mark is lighter than the primary accent mark. This mark symbolizes a stress on the syllable, but not as strong a stress as on the syllable with the primary accent mark next to it. For example, in the word *appetizer* [ap′ə tī′ zər], the third syllable has some stress, symbolized by the secondary accent mark, but the first syllable has the strongest stress, as shown by the primary accent mark.

Pronunciation Differences

The pronunciations given in dictionaries are considered the standard pronunciations, although some words can be pronounced more than one way, and both are considered correct. For example, consider the word *Caribbean* [kar′ ə bē′ ən, kə rib′ ē ən]. You will hear different pronunciations by English speakers worldwide. British, Canadian, Australian, and American speakers may not even understand each other at times due to different pronunciations of the same word. Even within a country, people do not sound the same. Regional differences are found throughout the United States; Texans, New Yorkers, and Californians do not always sound the same. Differences in pronunciations are also due to other factors, such as education and age. The dynamics of language make learning new words and learning about words an exciting enterprise.

MyReadingLab™: Improving Reading through Personalized Learning Experiences

In an ideal world, an instructor would have more time to work with each student individually to improve writing and reading skills with consistent challenges and rewards. Without that luxury, MyReadingLab offers a way to keep students focused and accelerate their progress using comprehensive pre-assignments and a powerful, adaptive study plan.

Flexible Enough to Fit Every Course Need

MyReadingLab can be set up to fit your specific course needs, whether you seek writing support to complement what you do in class, a way to easily administer many sections, or a self-paced environment for independent study.

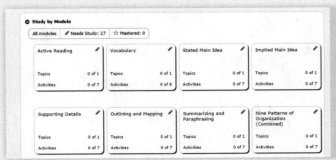

Learning in Context

In addition to distinct pre-loaded learning paths for reading/writing skills practice and reading level practice, MyReadingLab incorporates numerous activities for practice and readings from the accompanying textbook. This combination makes the connection between what's done in and out of the classroom more relevant to students.

NEW! Learning Tools for Student Engagement

Create an Engaging Classroom

Learning Catalytics is an interactive, student-response tool in MyReadingLab that uses students' smartphones, tablets, or laptops, allowing instructors to easily generate class discussion, guide lectures, and promote peer-to-peer learning with real-time analytics.

Build Multimedia Assignments

MediaShare allows students to easily post multimodal assignments for peer review and instructor feedback. In both face-to-face and online courses, MediaShare enriches the student learning experience by enabling contextual feedback to be provided quickly and easily.

Direct Access to MyLab

Users can link from any Learning Management System (LMS) to Pearson's MyReadingLab. Access MyLab assignments, rosters and resources, and synchronize MyLab grades with your LMS gradebook.

Visit www.myreadinglab.com for more information.

Active Vocabulary

General and Academic Words

Sixth Edition

Amy E. Olsen

Argosy University

PEARSON

Boston   Columbus   Indianapolis   New York   San Francisco   Amsterdam
Cape Town   Dubai   London   Madrid   Milan   Munich   Paris   Montréal   Toronto
Delhi   Mexico City   São Paulo   Sydney   Hong Kong   Seoul   Singapore   Taipei   Tokyo

Dedication

To those who inspire and lead active lives
Be it through books, travel, or sports and games

—Amy E. Olsen

Executive Editor: Matthew Wright
Program Manager: Eric Jorgensen
Product Marketing Manager: Jennifer Edwards
Field Marketing Manager: Mark Robinson
Media Editor: Kelsey Loveday
Digital Content Specialist: Julia Pomann
Senior Media Producer: Marisa Massaro
Project Manager: Rebecca Gilpin
Project Coordination, Text Design, and Electronic Page Makeup: Integra
Design Lead: Heather Scott
Cover Designer: Studio Montage
Cover Illustration: Svetlana Lukienko/Shutterstock
Senior Manufacturing Buyer: Roy L. Pickering, Jr.
Printer/Binder: RR Donnelley/Roanoke
Cover Printer: Lehigh-Phoenix Color/Hagerstown

Photo Credits: p. 10: Gerald Warnken, Jr.; **p. 13 (L):** Dan A. Tallorin; **p. 13 (R):** Milt Olsen; **p. 16:** Amy E. Olsen; **p. 22 (T):** Amy E. Olsen; **p. 22 (B):** Kris Rosenquist; **p. 24:** Amy E. Olsen; **p. 26:** Amy E. Olsen; **p. 30:** Amy E. Olsen; **p. 33:** Gerald Warnken, Jr.; **p. 37:** Amy E. Olsen; **p. 39:** Milt Olsen; **p. 42:** Pixbox77/Shutterstock; **p. 46:** Gerald Warnken, Jr; **p. 48:** Amy E. Olsen; **p. 54:** Amy E. Olsen; **p. 56:** Amy E. Olsen; **p. 57:** Amy E. Olsen; **p. 62:** Amy E. Olsen; **p. 65:** Gerald Warnken, Jr.; **p. 69:** Amy E. Olsen; **p. 73:** Amy E. Olsen; **p. 76:** Milt Olsen; **p. 78:** Amy E. Olsen; **p. 80 (T):** Amy E. Olsen; **p. 80 (B):** Gerald Warnken, Jr.; **p. 82 (T):** Gerald Warnken, Jr.; **p. 82:** Teo Boon Keng Alvin/Shutterstock; **p. 88:** Amy E. Olsen; **p. 91 (L):** Amy E. Olsen; **p. 91 (R):** Milt Olsen; **p. 96:** Amy E. Olsen; **p. 99:** Amy E. Olsen; **p. 103:** Amy E. Olsen; **p. 105 (T & L):** Milt Olsen; **p. 105 (B):** Amy E. Olsen; **p. 108:** Amy E. Olsen; **p. 109:** Amy E. Olsen; **p. 110 (L):** Gerald Warnken, Jr.; **p. 110 (R):** Amy E. Olsen; **p. 112:** Gerald Warnken, Jr.; **p. 114:** Amy E. Olsen; **p. 116:** Tony Olsen; **p. 117:** Milt Olsen; **p. 118:** Amy E. Olsen; **p. 120:** Amy E. Olsen; **p. 122:** Milt Olsen; **p. 129:** Amy E. Olsen; **p. 131:** Amy E. Olsen; **p. 133:** Amy E. Olsen; **p. 134:** Amy E. Olsen; **p. 136:** Studio 1One/Shutterstock; **p. 138:** Amy E. Olsen; **p. 140 (T):** Tony Olsen; **p. 140 (B):** Amy E. Olsen; **p. 142:** Tony Olsen; **p. 143:** Gerald Warnken, Jr.; **p. 146 (T):** Katy Tallorin; **p. 146 (B):** Amy E. Olsen; **p. 149:** Amy E. Olsen; **p. 152:** Amy E. Olsen; **p. 161:** Amy E. Olsen; **p. 163 (T):** Gerald Warnken, Jr.; **p. 163 (B):** Tony Olsen.

10 9 8 7 6 5 4 3 2 1—RRD—19 18 17 16

www.pearsonhighered.com

PEARSON

Student Edition ISBN 10:   0-13-411969-X
Student Edition ISBN 13: 978-0-13-411969-4

Contents

PART II Academic Words

Because students benefit greatly from increased word power, the study of vocabulary should be enjoyable. Unfortunately, vocabulary workbooks often lose sight of this goal. To help make the study of vocabulary an exciting and enjoyable part of college study, I have written *Active Vocabulary*.

The goal of this book—the second in a three-book interactive vocabulary series—is to make the study of vocabulary fun through a variety of thematic readings, self-tests, and interactive exercises. As a casual glimpse through the book will indicate, these activities involve writing, personal experience, art, and many other formats. The goal of these activities is simple: to utilize individual learning styles in order to help students learn new words in a large number of contexts.

Underlying the text's strong visual appeal is a central philosophy: an essential part of learning vocabulary is repeated exposure to a word. *Active Vocabulary* provides eight to ten exposures to each vocabulary word within the main chapters of the text plus additional coverage in the Review chapters and through the flash card and word map activities explained in the book. More opportunities for exposure can also be found in the Collaborative Activities and games in the Instructor's Manual.

Features New to This Edition

This sixth edition has several new features in response to instructor comments. The new materials have been employed to make the text more appealing to students and easier for instructors to use.

- **New Word Reactions Activity:** The Word Reactions activity asks students to monitor their responses to the vocabulary words by creating lists in different categories. The categories include words that a student especially likes, finds very useful, or considers hard to pronounce. There is also a space for students to create their own category. Making the lists will help students better connect with the vocabulary words because they will be closely thinking about different aspects of a word (its meaning, sound, applications to daily life). The activity also has the goal of making students more generally aware of words they come in contact with and their feelings about them. Instructors can use the lists to gauge what words may need extra instruction and for prompting class discussions.
- **Updated Content:** The Conversation Starters have been updated to provide new topics that give students a chance to chat using the vocabulary words from one chapter or for an entire section. The questions in the Conversation Starters are an excellent way to get students to orally use the vocabulary words in a casual setting. In the Getting Started chapter, the Using the Dictionary section has been updated with a new Guide Words Practice exercise and a new Multiple Meanings exercise. Additionally, information on dividing words into syllables has been added to the discussion on dictionary entries. The Completing Analogies section has an updated matching and fill-in-the-blank exercise.
- **New Readings and Words:** Three chapters have new readings, and the readings in two other chapters have been updated. Fourteen new words have been added to the text.

Content Overview

Active Vocabulary is an ideal text for both classroom and self-study. The sixteen main chapters follow a specific and consistent format.

- **Thematic Reading:** Because most vocabulary is acquired through reading, each chapter, with the exception of the Word Parts and Review Chapters, begins with a thematic reading that introduces ten vocabulary words in context. These readings come in a variety of formats, from newspaper reviews to online class assignments. The goal is to show that new words may be encountered anywhere. Rather than simply presenting a word list with definitions, students have the opportunity to discover the meanings of these new words via context clues.

  The themes for *Active Vocabulary* were chosen from areas most interesting to students of all ages and from disciplines that most students will encounter at some point in their college careers. In choosing the words, I've been guided by five factors: (1) relation to the chapter theme, (2) use in popular magazines, newspapers, novels, and textbooks, (3) occurrence in standardized lists and tests such as the Academic Word List, SAT, and GRE, (4) inclusion of word parts introduced in the text, and (5) my experiences teaching in reading and writing classrooms.

- **Predicting:** The second page of each chapter contains a Predicting activity that gives students the chance to figure out the meaning of each vocabulary word before looking at its definition. The Predicting section helps students learn the value of context clues in determining a word's meaning. While the text does offer information on dictionary use, I strongly advocate the use of context clues as one of the most active methods of vocabulary development.

- **Self-Tests:** Following the Predicting activity are three Self-Tests in various formats. With these tests, students can monitor their comprehension. The tests include text and sentence completion, true/false situations, matching, and analogies. Some tests employ context clue strategies such as synonyms and antonyms and general meaning. Critical-thinking skills are an important part of each test. (Answers to the Self-Tests appear in the Instructor's Manual.)

- **Word Visions:** The Word Visions activities give students the opportunity to connect the vocabulary words to visuals. The Word Visions are either located within the Self-Tests section or as an Interactive Exercise. The activities ask students to identify a vocabulary word represented in a drawing or photo or to use a photograph as inspiration to write sentences or a paragraph using the chapter's vocabulary words.

- **Word Wise:** Following the Self-Tests is the Word Wise section, which teaches a variety of skills that are helpful to vocabulary acquisition. There are six types of activities: Internet Activities, Context Clue Mini-Lessons, Collocations, Word Pairs, Connotations and Denotations, and Interesting Etymologies. Each activity is explained in the Getting Started section. By doing these activities and reading more about how words are used, students will get additional practice and insight into the words they are learning.

- **Interactive Exercise:** Following the Word Wise section is an Interactive Exercise, which asks the student to begin actively using the vocabulary words. The exercises may include writing, making lists, or answering questions. The Interactive Exercises give students the chance to really think about the meanings of the words, but, more importantly, they encourage students to begin using the words actively. Some instructors like to have their students do the Interactive Exercise in small groups (or pairs) and then have the groups share their responses with the whole class. (See the Instructor's Manual for more ideas on collaborative activities.)

- **Hint, Word Part Reminder, or Conversation Starters:** Each chapter includes a Hint, a Word Part Reminder, or Conversation Starters. The Hints cover tips for developing vocabulary, reading, or study skills; the Hints are brief and practical, and students will be able to make use of them in all of their college courses. The Word Part Reminders are short exercises that give students a chance to practice using a few of the word parts they have recently learned. The Conversation Starters are questions that ask students to use the words while talking with each other. The goal of the Conversation Starters is to get students using the words in daily life.
- **Word List:** The last page in a chapter contains a list of the vocabulary words with a pronunciation guide, the part of speech, and a brief definition for each. I wrote these definitions with the idea of keeping them simple and nontechnical. Some vocabulary texts provide complicated dictionary definitions that include words students do not know; I've tried to make the definitions as friendly and as useful as possible.
- **Words to Watch:** The final activity asks students to pick 3–5 words they may be having trouble with and to write their own sentences using the words. This section is an additional chance for students to grasp the meaning of a few words that may be difficult for them.

Additional Features

In addition to the thematic vocabulary chapters, *Active Vocabulary* includes a Pronunciation Guide, a Getting Started chapter, three Word Parts chapters, five Review chapters, a Glossary, a Flash Card section, a Word Map section, a Word Reactions section, and a Word List.

- **Pronunciation Guide:** At the front of the text is a Pronunciation Guide to help students understand the pronunciation symbols used in this book. The Guide also offers additional information on pronunciation issues.
- **Getting Started:** *Active Vocabulary* begins with an introductory chapter to familiarize students with some of the tools of vocabulary acquisition. The "Learning Objectives" serve to help students understand the goals of the text and to encourage them to see the benefits of studying vocabulary. The "Parts of Speech" section gives sample words and sentences for the eight parts of speech. "Using the Dictionary" provides an exercise for using guide words, dissects a sample dictionary entry, and offers a short exercise on multiple meanings. "Completing Analogies" explains how analogies work, provides sample analogies, and gives students analogy exercises to complete. This section will prepare students for the analogy Self-Tests contained in several chapters of the text. The "Benefits of Flash Cards and Word Maps" section explains the advantages of these study tools and encourages students to make flash cards and word maps beginning with Chapter 1. The "Word Wise Features" section provides background information for the various Word Wise activities.
- **Word Parts:** The three Word Parts chapters introduce prefixes, roots, and suffixes used throughout the book. Students learn the meanings of these forms, and sample words illustrate the forms. Self-Tests in each Word Parts chapter give students the opportunity to practice using the word parts.
- **Review Chapters:** Five Review chapters focus on the preceding three or four chapters. They divide the words into different activity groups and test students' cumulative knowledge. The words appear in test, written, visual, puzzle, and collaborative formats. These repeated and varied exposures increase the likelihood that the students will remember the words, not just for one chapter or test, but for life.
- **Glossary:** The Glossary lists all the vocabulary words, along with the part of speech and the definitions given in each chapter. Students may find it handy to refer to the Glossary when reviewing words from several chapters.

- **Create Your Own Flash Cards:** The "Create Your Own Flash Cards" section teaches students how to make and use flash cards. Students can use the cards for self-study. Additionally, instructors can use them for the supplemental activities and games that are provided in the Instructor's Manual.
- **Make Your Own Word Maps:** The "Make Your Own Word Maps" section teaches students how to make word maps that focus on learning the definition, synonyms, and antonyms for a word. Students can use the maps as another strategy for self-study.
- **Word Reactions:** The "Word Reactions" page is new to this edition. This activity allows students to record their reactions to the vocabulary words by creating lists in different categories. The goal of this feature is to make students more connected to the vocabulary words and their meanings by carefully thinking about how they respond to a word. (See the Instructor's Manual for ideas on ways to use the lists through activities that include conversation, writing, technology, and movement.)
- **Word List:** The list, located at the end of the text, presents all the vocabulary words and the page numbers on which the definitions are given. A list of the word parts from the Word Parts Chapters is also included, with page references.

The Teaching and Learning Package

Each component of the teaching and learning package for *Active Vocabulary* has been carefully crafted to maximize the main text's value.

- **New MyReadingLab Program:** The Self-Tests from each chapter in the text have been incorporated into Pearson's online learning system, MyReadingLab. This exciting new component of the text gives students an additional way to interact with the words. Another benefit of the MyReadingLab program is the automatic scoring of a student's answers, which provides the student and instructor with quick feedback as to how a student is doing. For more information on this feature visit www.myreadinglab.com.
- **Instructor's Manual (ISBN: 0-13-411973-8) and Test Bank (ISBN: 0-13-411982-7):** The Instructor's Manual includes options for additional Collaborative Activities and games. The collaborative section explains ways students can share their work on the Interactive Exercises and on the Word Reactions feature in pairs, in small groups, or with the whole class. Ideas for other collaborative activities using different learning styles are also offered. The games section presents games that can be used with individual chapters or for review of several chapters. Some of the games are individual; others are full-class activities. Some games have winners, and some are just for fun. The games may involve acting, drawing, or writing. The Collaborative Activities and games give students the opportunity to use the words in conversational settings and a chance to work with others. The Test Bank provides quizzes for each chapter, as well as full-book tests that can be used as final exams.

For Additional Reading and Reference

The Longman Basic Skills Package

In addition to the book-specific supplements discussed above, many other skills-based supplements are available for both instructors and students. All of these supplements are available either at no additional cost or at greatly reduced prices.

- **The Dictionary Deal.** Two dictionaries can be shrink-wrapped with *Active Vocabulary* at a nominal fee. *The New American Webster Handy College Dictionary* is a paperback reference text with more than 100,000 entries. *Merriam-Webster's Collegiate Dictionary,* eleventh edition, is a hardback reference with a citation file of more than 14.5 million examples of English words drawn from actual use. For more information on how to shrink-wrap a dictionary with your text, please contact your Pearson publishing representative.

- **Longman Vocabulary Web Site.** For additional vocabulary-related resources, visit our free vocabulary Web site at http://www.ablongman.com/vocabulary.

Acknowledgments

I want to thank the following reviewers for their helpful suggestions as the sixth edition took shape: Yolanda Cooper, Bossier Parish Community College; Robert Mann, Des Moines Area Community College Urban Campus; Lisa Kovacs Morgan, UC San Diego English Language Institute; Mark Poupard, UC San Diego English Language Institute; Carolyn Smith, Baton Rouge Community College; Pamela Walsh, Schenectady County Community College.

Additionally, I am grateful to Eric Jorgensen, Program Manager at Pearson, for his help and dedication in preparing this edition. I am also thankful to Eric Stano, Vice President and Editorial Director in English at Pearson, for his continuous support of the vocabulary series. Thanks also to the Production, Marketing, and Supplement departments of Pearson for their thoughtful work on various aspects of the book. I am grateful to several colleagues and students for insightful comments. I thank my family for their loyal support. Lastly, I sincerely appreciate my husband for his comments on questions he never thought he would be asked.

I am pleased that this edition continues to combine traditional and innovative approaches to vocabulary study. I am delighted to present the sixth edition of *Active Vocabulary,* a book that makes learning vocabulary fun and meaningful.

—AMY E. OLSEN

Also Available

Book 1 of the Vocabulary Series:

Interactive Vocabulary: General Words, by Amy E. Olsen

Book 3 of the Vocabulary Series:

Academic Vocabulary: Academic Words, by Amy E. Olsen

A reader that combines a holistic and specific-skill approach with thought-provoking readings and activities that ask students to connect with what they read:

Reading Now, by Amy E. Olsen

To the Student

This book is designed to make learning vocabulary fun. You will increase the benefits of this book if you keep a few points in mind:

1. **Interact with the words.** Each main chapter contains eight to ten exposures to a word, and your instructor may introduce one or two additional activities. If you're careful in your reading and thorough in doing the activities for each chapter, learning the words will be fun and easy.

2. **Appreciate the importance of words.** The words for the readings were picked from popular magazines and newspapers, novels, lists of words likely to appear on standardized tests (such as SAT and GRE), and textbooks from a variety of academic disciplines. These are words you will encounter in everyday life and in the classroom. Learning these words will help you be a more informed citizen and make your academic life much richer. Even if you don't currently have an interest in one of the readings, keep an open mind: the words may appear in the article you read in tomorrow's newspaper or on an exam in one of next semester's classes. The readings also come in different formats as a reminder that you can learn new vocabulary anywhere—from a Web site to a newspaper article.

3. **Find your preferred learning style.** This book aims to provide exercises for all types of learners—visual, aural, and interpersonal. But only you can say which learning style works best for you. See which activities (drawings, acting, matching, completing stories) you like most, and replicate those activities when they aren't part of the chapter.

4. **Value critical thinking.** The variety of exercise formats you will find in the following pages make the book fun to work with and build a range of critical-thinking skills. For example, the analogies will help you see relationships between words, the fill-in-the-blank formats will aid you in learning to put words into context, and the true/false Self-Tests will focus your attention on whether words are used correctly in a sentence. Each type of activity will develop your critical-thinking skills while building your vocabulary.

5. **Remember that learning is fun.** Don't make a chore out of learning new words, or any other new skill for that matter. If you enjoy what you're doing, you're more likely to welcome the information and to retain it.

Enjoy your journey through *Active Vocabulary!*

—AMY E. OLSEN

Part I

General Words

Learning Objectives

The ultimate goals of *Active Vocabulary* are to increase your vocabulary and build your critical-thinking skills, and you will attain these goals by achieving a number of learning objectives. Each exercise in *Active Vocabulary* will help you to master one or more of the following learning objectives:

LO 1 Recognize and use context clues to determine the meanings of new words.

LO 2 Apply new vocabulary to writing and speaking situations.

LO 3 Appreciate that words can have multiple meanings.

LO 4 Understand relationships between words.

LO 5 Recognize word parts and use them to decode the meanings of unfamiliar words.

LO 6 Use the vocabulary words to respond to images.

LO 7 Employ a pronunciation key to correctly pronounce words.

LO 8 Create and use flash cards and word maps as learning aids.

Look for the "Learning Objective" icon in the Review Chapters to identify exercises that will help you master each objective. Though only one or two learning objectives are identified for most of the exercises, you may discover that you are using skills found in other objectives.

Parts of Speech

There are eight parts of speech. A word's part of speech is based on how the word is used in a sentence. Words can, therefore, be more than one part of speech. For an example, note how the word *punch* is used below.

nouns: (n.) name a person, place, or thing
> EXAMPLES: Ms. Lopez, New Orleans, lamp, warmth
> *Ms. Lopez* enjoyed her *trip* to *New Orleans,* where she bought a beautiful *lamp.* The *warmth* of the *sun* filled *Claire* with *happiness.* I drank five *cups* of the orange *punch.*

pronouns: (pron.) take the place of a noun
> EXAMPLES: I, me, you, she, he, it, her, we, they, my, which, that, anybody, everybody
> *Everybody* liked the music at the party. *It* was the kind that made people want to dance. *They* bought a new car, *which* hurt their bank account.

verbs: (v.) express an action or state of being
> EXAMPLES: enjoy, run, think, read, dance, am, is, are, was, were
> Lily *read* an interesting book yesterday. I *am* tired. He *is* an excellent student. She *punched* the bully.

adjectives: (adj.) modify (describe or explain) a noun or pronoun
> EXAMPLES: pretty, old, two, expensive, red, small
> The *old* car was covered with *red* paint on *one* side. The *two* women met for lunch at an *expensive* restaurant. The *punch* bowl was *empty* soon after Uncle Al got to the party.

adverbs: (adv.) modify a verb, an adjective, or another adverb
> EXAMPLES: very, shortly, first, too, soon, quickly, finally, furthermore, however
> We will meet *shortly* after one o'clock. The *very* pretty dress sold *quickly.* I liked her; *however,* there was something strange about her.

prepositions: (prep.) are placed before a noun or pronoun to create a phrase that relates to other parts of the sentence

EXAMPLES: after, around, at, before, by, from, in, into, of, off, on, through, to, up, with
He told me to be *at* his house *in* the afternoon. You must go *through* all the steps to do the job.

conjunctions: (conj.) join words or other sentence elements and show a relationship between the connected items

EXAMPLES: and, but, or, nor, for, so, yet, after, although, because, if, since, than, when
I went to the movies, *and* I went to dinner on Tuesday. I will not go to the party this weekend *because* I have to study. I don't want to hear your reasons *or* excuses.

interjections: (interj.) show surprise or emotion

EXAMPLES: oh, hey, wow, ah, ouch
Oh, I forgot to do my homework! *Wow,* I got an A on the test!

Using the Dictionary

There will be times when you need to use a dictionary for one of its many features; becoming familiar with dictionary **entries** will make using a dictionary more enjoyable. The words in a dictionary are arranged alphabetically. The words on a given page are signaled by **guide words** at the top of the page. If the word you are looking for comes alphabetically between these two words, then your word is on that page. When using online dictionaries, you will simply type in the word you are looking for, so guide words will not be important, but the other features of an entry remain the same.

Guide Words Practice

Put a checkmark next to the words that would be found on a page with the guide words below. Check the words that alphabetically come between the guide words *cadet* and *cairn*.

Page number → 245 cadet/cairn ← Guide words

_____ cage	_____ Cairo	_____ Caicos Islands
_____ cake	_____ Caesar, Julius	_____ cacao
_____ cadmium	_____ caddy	_____ cafeteria

Dictionary Entry

Most dictionaries contain the following information in an entry:

- The word divided into **syllables**—dots separate a word into syllables. In the sample entry on the next page, *confirm* is divided into two syllables. The word *immediately* would be divided in an entry as im•me•di•ate•ly, showing that it contains five syllables. Seeing a word divided into syllables can help in pronouncing it. The syllable divisions are also helpful in learning how to spell a word. See the examples below:

  back•rest = one word
  back seat = two words
  back•yard also back yard = can be written as one or two words
- The **pronunciation**—symbols show how a word should be spoken, including how the word is divided into syllables and where the stress should be placed on a word. The Pronunciation Guide for this book is located on page i. The guide shows the symbols used to indicate the sound of a word. Every dictionary has a pronunciation method, and a pronunciation guide or key is usually found in the front pages, with a partial key at the bottom of each page. The differences in the pronunciation systems used by dictionaries are usually slight.

- The **part of speech**—usually abbreviated, such as *n.* for noun, *v.* for verb, and *adj.* for adjective. A key to these abbreviations and others is usually found in the front of the dictionary.
- The **definition**—usually the most common meaning is listed first followed by other meanings.
- An **example of the word in a sentence**—the sentence is usually in italics and follows each meaning.
- **Synonyms** and **antonyms**—*synonyms* are words with similar meanings, and *antonyms* are words with opposite meanings. (You should also consider owning a **thesaurus**, a book that lists synonyms and antonyms.)
- The **etymology**—the history of a word, usually including the language(s) it came from.
- The **spelling of different forms** of the word—these forms may include unusual plurals (for example, mouse and mice) and verb tenses, especially irregular forms (for example, rise, rose, risen).

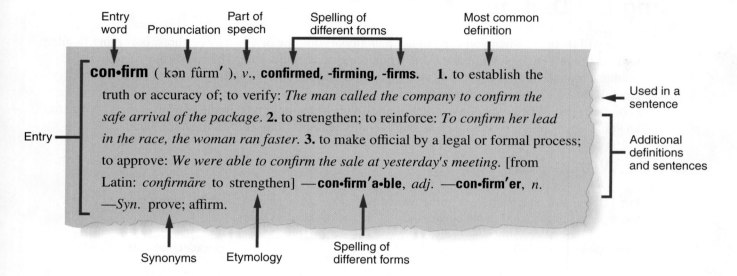

Despite the popularity of online dictionaries, it can still be handy to own a paper version. When choosing a dictionary, take the time to look at different dictionaries to see what appeals to you. Dictionaries come in several sizes and are made for different purposes. First read some of the entries to see if the definitions make sense to you. See which of the features above are used in the dictionary. Is it important to you to be able to study the etymology of a word? Would you like sample sentences? Some dictionaries have illustrations in the margins. Decide if that is a feature you would use. Check to see if the print is large enough for you to read easily.

Decide on how you will use this dictionary. Do you want a paperback dictionary to put in your backpack? Or is this going to be the dictionary for your desk and a large hardback version would be the better choice? Several disciplines have specialized dictionaries with meanings that apply to those fields, such as law or medicine. There are also bilingual dictionaries, such as French/English or Spanish/English, that can be helpful for school or travel. Take time in picking out a dictionary because a good dictionary will be a companion for years to come. A few dictionaries to consider are *Merriam-Webster's Collegiate Dictionary*, *The American Heritage Dictionary*, *The Random House College Dictionary,* and *The Oxford Dictionary*.

In general, when you are reading, try to use context clues—the words around the word you don't know—to first figure out the meaning of a word; but if you are still in doubt, don't hesitate to refer to a dictionary for the exact definition. Don't forget that dictionaries also contain more than definitions and are an essential reference source for any student.

Entry Identification

Label the parts of the following entry.

① **②** **③** **④** **⑤**

a•ble (ā′ bəl) *adj.* **a•bler, a•blest.** 1. having the necessary power, skill, or qualifications to do something: *She was able to read music.* **⑥**

⑦ 2. having or showing unusual talent, intelligence, skill, or knowledge: *Washington was an able leader.* [1275–1325; ME < MF < L **⑧** *habilis* easy to handle, adaptable = *hab(ēre)* to have, hold + *ilis* –ile] *Syn.* apt, talented.

⑨

1. _____
2. _____
3. _____
4. _____
5. _____
6. _____
7. _____
8. _____
9. _____

Multiple Meanings

As the two sample entries show, a word can have more than one meaning. When reading, examine how a word is used in a sentence to determine which of its multiple meanings fits with the way the writer has used it. Read the examples below, and indicate whether the sentence matches meaning 1, 2, or 3 for the sample entry *confirm*.

1. Reporters should confirm the information they are given before writing a story.
   Meaning: _____

2. The ceremony to confirm Reyes as the new Secretary of State will be held tomorrow.
   Meaning: _____

3. When Ann made the Dean's List after her first semester, it helped to confirm her parents' belief that she would do well in college.
   Meaning: _____

4. The sale of the property will be confirmed when the papers are signed tomorrow.
   Meaning: _____

5. The phone records confirm that the man was at work during the time of the robbery.
   Meaning: _____

6. The candidate's success in the debate confirmed her lead in the polls.
   Meaning: _____

Completing Analogies

An **analogy** shows a relationship between words. Working with analogies helps one to see connections between items, which is a crucial critical-thinking skill. Analogies are written as follows:

big : large :: fast : quick

The colon (:) means *is to*. The analogy reads big *is to* large as fast *is to* quick. To complete analogies

1. find a relationship between the first pair of words
2. look for a similar relationship in another set of words

In the example above, *big* and *large* have similar meanings; they are synonyms. *Fast* and *quick* also have similar meanings, so the relationship between the four words uses synonyms.

Common relationships used in analogies (with examples) include

synonyms (trip : journey)   grammatical structure (shaking : shivering)

antonyms (real : fake)   cause and effect (step in a puddle : get wet)

examples (strawberry : fruit)   sequences (turn on car : drive)

part to a whole (handle : cup)   an object to a user or its use (spatula : chef)

Analogies in this book come in matching and fill-in-the-blank forms. Try the following analogies for practice.

Matching

1. old : young ::   _____   a. preface : book

2. clip coupons : go shopping ::   _____   b. put on shoes : take a walk

3. peel : banana ::   _____   c. low wages : strike

4. no rain : drought ::   _____   d. rested : tired

Fill-in-the-Blank

writer	passion	abduct	sadly

5. frozen : chilled :: kidnap : _____

6. interrupting : rude :: embracing : _____

7. slow : slowly :: sad : _____

8. baton : conductor :: computer : _____

Answers

1. To figure out this analogy, first one needs to see that *old* and *young* are opposites, or **antonyms**. Next look at the choices and see if another pair of words are antonyms, and yes, *rested* and *tired* are opposites. The answer is d.
2. A person would *clip coupons* and then *go shopping*, so there is a **sequence** of events. Of the choices, one would *put on shoes* and then *take a walk*, another sequence. The answer is b.
3. A *peel* is a part of a *banana*, while a *preface* is part of a *book*, so the connection is **part to a whole**. The answer is a.
4. When an area gets *no rain*, it can lead to a *drought*, and when people get paid *low wages*, they can go on *strike*. The connection among these pairs is **cause and effect**. The answer is c.
5. *Frozen* and *chilled* have similar meanings; they are **synonyms**. To solve the analogy, pick a word that has a similar meaning to *kidnap*, which would be *abduct*.
6. *Interrupting* a person is **an example** of a *rude* behavior. *Embracing* is an example of another type of behavior; in this case, it fits as an example of *passion*.
7. *Slow* is an adjective, and *slowly* is an adverb; *sad* is an adjective, and *sadly* is an adverb. This analogy works by using the same **grammatical structure** between the words.
8. A *baton* is used by a *conductor*. Who uses a *computer?* Among the choices, *writer* obviously fits. The relationship here is **object to user**.

Sometimes you may come up with a relationship between the first two words that makes sense but doesn't fit any of the choices. Look at the choices and the two words again to see if you can find a way any four words fit together. Also do any obvious matches first, and with fewer choices it will be easier to spot the harder connections. Doing analogies can be fun as you begin to make clever associations and see word relationships in new ways. Finding word connections will help your brain make other connections in areas as diverse as writing essays, doing math problems, and arranging travel plans. Analogies are just another way to exercise your thinking skills.

Try a few more analogies, and check your answers on page 36 to see how you did.

Matching

1. frame : picture ::   _____   a. microscope : biologist

2. scissors : stylist ::   _____   b. silent : quiet

3. varied : different ::   _____   c. lose a game : depressed

4. find keys : happy ::   _____   d. mouth : face

Fill-in-the-Blank

| joy | spice | thaw | geese |

5. add detergent : press start :: remove from freezer : _____

6. complex : simple :: sadness : _____

7. foot : feet :: goose : _____

8. rose : flower :: ginger : _____

Benefits of Flash Cards and Word Maps

There are several benefits to using flash cards and word maps to help you study vocabulary words.

Creating The first benefit comes from just making the cards or maps. When you make a card, you will practice writing the word and its definition. You may also write a sentence using the word, record its part of speech, or draw a picture of the word. See the section "Create Your Own Flash Cards" on page 170 for ideas on how to make flash cards. When you make a word map, you will practice writing the word, its definition, and a synonym and antonym for the word. See the section "Make Your Own Word Maps" on page 172 for examples. Creating the cards or maps allows for a personal experience with the words, which makes learning the words easier.

Working With Others Another benefit is that using the cards or maps can lead to collaborative activities. When you ask a friend, family member, or classmate to quiz you on the words, you get the chance to work with someone else, which many people enjoy. You may even establish a study group with the friends you find from quizzing each other.

Evaluating Your Learning A third benefit is that the cards or maps serve as pre-tests that let you evaluate how well you know a word. When a friend quizzes you, ask him or her to go over the words you miss several times. As the stack of flash cards or maps with words you don't know gets smaller, you know that the words are becoming part of your vocabulary. You know that you are prepared to face a word on a quiz or test when you can correctly give the definition several times.

Making and using the flash cards and word maps should be fun. Enjoy the process of learning new words. Turn to the back of the book now to review the directions for both methods, and you will be ready to make cards or maps beginning with Chapter 1. Experiment with using both methods early in the term to see which method best helps you learn the words.

Word Wise Features

The Word Wise boxes share information on different areas related to vocabulary. There are six types of features.

Internet Activities suggest ways to use technology to enhance your learning experience.

Context Clue Mini-Lessons provide different types of context-clue situations and give you the opportunity to practice using each type. *Context* means the words surrounding a specific word that give clues to that word's meaning. When you encounter a word whose meaning you don't know, keep reading the passage, looking for clues to help you figure out the meaning. These clues might be in the same sentence as the unknown words or in a sentence that comes before or after the word. Look for these types of clues in a passage:

Synonym—word that has a similar meaning to the unknown word

Antonym—word that means the opposite of the unknown word

General meaning—the meaning of the sentence or passage as a whole that could clarify the meaning of the unknown word

Example—a single item (or a list of items) that shows the meaning of the unknown word

A way to remember the four types of context clues is to use the acronym SAGE (synonym, antonym, general meaning, example). Sage also means wise or showing wisdom, so you can feel smart about using this mnemonic device. Each type of context clue has a mini-lesson, and a final lesson combines the methods.

Though more than a clue, keep watch for times when writers provide the definition of a word right after using it. The definition may be in parentheses or come after a comma. In a textbook, the definition may be highlighted in the margin or in a footnote. Writers usually provide a definition when the word they are using is a technical term or they feel the word would be an uncommon one for their readers.

You will not find a context clue every time you encounter a word you don't know, but being aware of context clues will help you determine the meaning of many new words and make reading more enjoyable.

Collocations show ways words are used together. The groupings can come in several forms, such as a verb with a noun (*commit* a *crime*), an adjective with a noun (*handsome stranger*), or a verb with a preposition (*come over*). Learning collocations will help you understand common ways to use the words you are studying. Sentences with the collocations in italics for some of the vocabulary words in this text are spread throughout the chapters. To become more familiar with collocations, look and listen for other repeated word combinations in the materials you read, in the phrases people use when speaking, and as you do the self-tests in this book.

Word Pairs illustrate how some words are often used near each other. Learning word pairs can help you to better remember both words. Some words are pairs because the items they represent are often used together, such as peanut butter and jelly. Other word pairs are opposites that are often found together when describing objects, actions, or people (such as "My friends are as different as night and day"). Word pairs are presented in several chapters with sample sentences to show how the words can be used near each other.

Connotations and Denotations examine reactions to a word. A **denotation** is "the explicit or direct meaning of a word." This is the kind of definition you would find in the dictionary. A **connotation** is "the suggestive meaning of a word beyond its literal definition." This is the emotional response you have to a word. A mnemonic device for remembering the difference between the two is that denotation begins with a "d," and it is the dictionary or direct meaning, both beginning with a "d."

It is important to realize that words have two kinds of meanings because careful writers use both kinds. You, as a writer and reader, want to make sure you are clearly expressing your point and understanding another writer's ideas by recognizing how words are used. Some connotations are personal reactions. For example, *seclusion* in Chapter 7 means "solitude; a sheltered or isolated place." Depending on your personality or current living conditions, you might picture *seclusion* as a wonderful chance to be alone and relax without all the chaos surrounding you; or if you hate being by yourself, you may envision it as a kind of torture separating you from friends and family. Other connotations have broader emotional responses. If you wanted to describe a thin person, you could use the words *slender* or *scrawny*. What do you picture in your mind for each word? Talk to your classmates about their images. Are they similar? Some words have positive connotations that people feel good about, and other words have negative connotations that turn people off. Not all words have strong connotations. For most people a pencil is a pencil, and there isn't much to get excited about. But other words can bring out strong feelings, such as *proud*. The Connotations and Denotations lessons look at some of the vocabulary words in this text and the differences in their meanings.

Interesting Etymologies present notable word histories. Some of the histories use the word parts presented in the three Word Parts chapters of the text. Learning the history of a word can help you to remember its meaning.

Chapter 1

On Campus

Study Skills

College can bring several challenges, but learning how to study effectively can make your life easier. Three important points to consider are place, time, and attitude.

First, you need a comfortable place to study. If
5 you can't focus on what you are reading, that usually **indicates** the need to find a new study location. Consider finding a quiet space on campus, such as the school library. You don't want to be distracted by noises (e.g., roommates talking or a television show). You should even
10 consider turning your cell phone off to **enable** you to fully concentrate. Prepare a study bag that is always ready to go to the library or other quiet location. Basic items to keep in a study bag include a ruler, calculator, paper, pens, and pencils. Throw in the appropriate notes and books for a
15 particular study session, and you are ready to go. If you are doing research or writing, a study spot should provide access to a laptop or the college's computers.

Once you have a study spot, make study time a central part of your day. To **implement** a study plan, get a
20 large calendar. Write the dates of your exams and due dates for papers on it. Also put your study times on the calendar. Put the calendar by your bed or in the kitchen where you can check it daily to see what assignments are coming up. Pay attention to your body to see when you feel the most alert and arrange your study times within these periods. Decide if you are the **zealous** night owl whose mind ignites once the sun goes down, or whether you concentrate better soon after waking up. Set aside at
25 least two hours every day. To make studying a habit, it can help to study during the same two hours each day. If your schedule varies, **intermittent** study periods also work. Four twenty- to thirty-minute study periods throughout a day can be used to review notes or to make a quick draft of a paper. When learning new **terminology**, studying words in ten- to fifteen-minute segments each day works better than studying the same words for ninety minutes once a week.

30 Finally, you need the right attitude to study successfully. People often **undermine** their study efforts by being stressed. People learn better if they are rested and relaxed. Go into each study session with a positive attitude. If you think the reading material will be interesting, you are more likely to find it so. If you walk into a classroom with the **assurance** that you will do well on a test, you are more likely to succeed than coming in filled with doubts. If you happen to do poorly, don't **berate**
35 yourself. Severely criticizing yourself to the point where you want to give up will not help you study better. Instead look at what went wrong. Maybe you needed to study more or you read the questions too fast. Work to do better in the future. Also, don't let **apathy** derail your planning. We all get bored at times, but procrastination usually leads to inferior work. Remind yourself of your goals for attending college as a way to motivate yourself. With efficient study skills, you can always walk onto
40 campus with confidence.

Predicting

For each set, write the definition on the line next to the word to which it belongs. If you are unsure, return to the reading, and underline any context clues you find. After you've made your predictions, check your answers against the Word List at the end of the chapter. Place a checkmark in the box next to each word whose definition you missed. These are the words you'll want to study closely.

Set One

enthusiastic	to put into practice	reveals	irregular	to permit

❑ 1. **indicates** (line 6) _____

❑ 2. **enable** (line 10) _____

❑ 3. **implement** (line 19) _____

❑ 4. **zealous** (line 23) _____

❑ 5. **intermittent** (line 26) _____

Set Two

self-confidence	to weaken or damage	to criticize	lack of interest

the words belonging to a specialized subject

❑ 6. **terminology** (line 28) _____

❑ 7. **undermine** (line 30) _____

❑ 8. **assurance** (line 33) _____

❑ 9. **berate** (line 34) _____

❑ 10. **apathy** (line 37) _____

Self-Tests

MyReadingLab Visit Chapter 1: On Campus in MyReadingLab to complete the Self-Test activities.

1 Match each term with its synonym in Set One and its antonym in Set Two.

Synonyms

Set One

_____	1. terminology	a. periodic
_____	2. enable	b. reveal
_____	3. implement	c. vocabulary
_____	4. intermittent	d. apply
_____	5. indicate	e. allow

Antonyms

Set Two

_____	6. undermine	f. bored
_____	7. assurance	g. praise
_____	8. berate	h. enthusiasm
_____	9. apathy	i. uncertainty
_____	10. zealous	j. strengthen

2 Circle the correct word to complete each sentence.

1. The day was supposed to be filled with (zealous, intermittent) showers, so we cancelled the picnic.

2. Spending a semester in Chile will (berate, enable) me to improve my Spanish faster than studying here in the United States.

3. I give you my (apathy, assurance) that the work will be done on time and be of the highest quality.

4. My friend was jealous of my relationship, so he tried to (undermine, implement) it by telling my girlfriend that I was seen kissing another woman.

5. I enjoy leading tours for children. They are so (intermittent, zealous); they want to see and do everything.

6. The (apathy, terminology) for my chemistry class is all new to me. I have had to really study the words to make sure I am doing the right things in the lab.

7. All the phone calls this week (indicate, enable) that we will have a large turnout for the book club meeting on Friday.

8. We will be able to (implement, berate) the new communication plan as soon as the cell phones arrive and we can distribute them to all of the staff.

9. When I was young, my mother always had to (berate, undermine) me to clean my room; now that I have my own apartment, I want to keep it clean.

10. The crowd's (assurance, apathy) did not inspire the players to try harder once they were behind by twenty points.

3 Complete the sentences using the vocabulary words. Use each word once.

VOCABULARY LIST

enabled	apathy	assurance	intermittent	berate
implement	indicate	zealous	undermine	terminology

1. I was worried about my cousin's _____; she did not feel like doing anything for two months after her dog died.

2. Getting a scholarship _____ me to go to college without having to work two jobs or take out a large loan.

3. The teacher had to _____ several students when they failed to do their homework three class sessions in a row.

4. The bank highlighted certain lines to _____ where I needed to sign my loan papers.

5. Once I learned the _____ at my new job, it was much easier to understand my boss when she asked me to do something.

6. With my son's _____ that he would go to the airport to pick up his sister, I was able to attend the meeting without any worries.

7. The _____ student went to the library to read more about advertising after learning a few techniques in his marketing class.

8. The _____ I can't do without in the kitchen is a whisk.

9. A couple of bad test results can _____ a student's confidence and lead to further poor performances.

10. My brother takes a(n) _____ interest in my art career; he calls me every five months or so to see what I am working on.

Word Visions

Identify the two vocabulary words represented in the photos.

1. _____

2. _____

Word Wise

Context Clue Mini-Lesson 1

Context clues can come in several forms. See page 8 for more information on the various types of context clues. The mini-lessons spread throughout this text give you a chance to practice looking for context clues by focusing on specific types of clues. This lesson features synonyms—words that have a similar meaning to the unknown word. In the paragraph below, circle the synonyms you find for the underlined words and write them on the lines that follow the paragraph.

I was having a good time at the party chatting with old friends and meeting new people. I met one <u>affable</u> man who had me laughing in seconds. He was so friendly that I felt like I had known him for years. Unfortunately, later in the evening he began to <u>chastise</u> me for eating cookies. He said he was scolding me because he cared about my health, but I knew a couple of cookies weren't going to hurt me. I wasn't going to be <u>compliant</u>, and I told him I was not the obedient type who did whatever people told her. He got angry and began yelling at me. My <u>elation</u> in meeting him quickly disappeared; the joy I had felt in first talking to him became a distant memory.

The Synonym

1. Affable _____

2. Chastise _____

3. Compliant _____

4. Elation _____

Interactive Exercise

Supply two examples for each who, what, why, when, and where question.

1. Who has enabled you to be successful in college or in a sport?

   _____

   _____

2. Who do you feel usually displays assurance (someone you know or a famous person)?

   _____

   _____

3. What could undermine a person's confidence?

   _____

   _____

4. What things are done intermittently?

   _____

   _____

5. Why would a person have to learn new terminology?

   _____

   _____

6. Why might a person berate oneself?

   _____

   _____

7. When would a person exhibit zealous behavior?

   _____

   _____

8. When would a company have to implement a new plan?

   _____

   _____

9. Where have you seen apathy displayed?

   _____

   _____

10. Where would be a romantic place to indicate your fondness for a person?

   _____

   _____

HINT

Flash Cards

Flash cards are a great way to study vocabulary. Turn to the "Create Your Own Flash Cards" section at the end of this book to read about ways to make and use flash cards. Remember to carry your flash cards with you and study for at least a few minutes each day. Also ask friends and family members to quiz you using the flash cards.

Word List

apathy
[ap′ ə thē]
n. lack of interest; absence or suppression of emotion or excitement

assurance
[ə shoor′ əns]
n. 1. self-confidence; certainty
2. a guarantee; a pledge or promise

berate
[bi rāt′]
v. to scold harshly; to criticize

enable
[en ā′ bəl]
v. to make possible; to permit

implement
[im′ plə mənt]
v. to apply; to put into practice
n. a tool or utensil

indicate
[in′ di kāt′]
v. 1. to be a sign of; to show the need for; to reveal
2. to point out or point to

intermittent
[in′ tər mit′ nt]
adj. stopping and beginning again; periodic; irregular

terminology
[tûr′ mə nol′ ə jē]
n. the words belonging to a specialized subject; the study of terms for particular subjects; vocabulary

undermine
[un′ dər mīn′, un′ dər mīn′]
v. 1. to weaken or damage (such as health or morale) by small stages
2. to weaken or cause to collapse by removing basic supports

zealous
[zel′ əs]
adj. enthusiastic; eager; passionate

Words to Watch

Which words would you like to practice with a bit more? Pick 3–5 words to study, and list them below. Write the word and its definition, and compose your own sentence using the word correctly. This extra practice could be the final touch to learning a word.

Word	Definition	Your Sentence
1. _____	_____	_____
_____	_____	_____
2. _____	_____	_____
_____	_____	_____
3. _____	_____	_____
_____	_____	_____
4. _____	_____	_____
_____	_____	_____
5. _____	_____	_____
_____	_____	_____

Chapter 2

Relationships

Solving Conflicts

NEWS

Communicating Effectively

As the term starts, opportunities arise to meet new people and to foster existing relationships. We can mainly expect to find **amiable** people who want to get along with one another. We will also encounter situations for possible conflicts, whether at school, work, or home. Conflicts happen, even with those we are close to, because people have different attitudes as to appropriate behaviors. Anger and frustration, however, need not win. To solve conflicts keep a few key points in mind.

1. Think carefully before making a comment. Imagine opening the refrigerator prepared to enjoy a slice of delicious leftover pizza. What you discover is that your roommate has eaten all four slices. This is a situation where you need to **restrain** the urge to call your roommate a "thief" or "hog." Holding back an initial angry response usually leads to a more positive outcome. You shouldn't be **submissive** and let your roommate eat all the food, but you need to judge how to effectively communicate your anger.

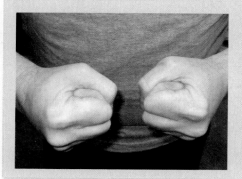

2. Be direct about an issue that is bothering you. You don't want to **imply** that a slice of pizza would be a tasty dinner. Your roommate might not pick up on your true meaning and simply suggest ordering a pizza. Directly state that you were looking forward to the leftover pizza and that you are upset that your roommate ate all four slices. If you want **serenity** in a relationship, be clear about matters that trouble you.

3. Consider ways to **compromise** that will please each person. It likely won't work to make an **arbitrary** decision that all food on the top shelf is yours and your roommate should never touch it. Make a **commitment** to work with each other to find a solution that will satisfy both people. If your roommate had eaten two slices and left you two, would you have been happy? If so, you could agree that you will share all leftovers and refrain from finishing any whole bag or box of food.

Changes can be difficult to make, so plan to **exemplify** the type of behavior you want to see. Displaying the agreed on behavior makes you a model for others, which usually leads to a successful outcome.

Of course, making any plan work means dealing with **dependable** people who can be trusted to follow through. Sometimes personalities can be so different or conflicts grow so large that outside help is needed to solve a problem. For those situations, stop by the Health Center to talk with a counselor about additional ways to resolve conflicts.

Guest column by Monique Martinez, Health Center director

Predicting

For each set, write the definition on the line next to the word to which it belongs. If you are unsure, return to the reading, and underline any context clues you find. After you've made your predictions, check your answers against the Word List at the end of the chapter. Place a checkmark in the box next to each word whose definition you missed. These are the words you'll want to study closely.

Set One

to hold back	agreeable	passive	peacefulness	to state indirectly

❑ 1. **amiable** (line 4) _____

❑ 2. **restrain** (line 21) _____

❑ 3. **submissive** (line 25) _____

❑ 4. **imply** (line 30) _____

❑ 5. **serenity** (line 38) _____

Set Two

responsible	a promise	determined by impulse	to cooperate	to represent

❑ 6. **compromise** (line 40) _____

❑ 7. **arbitrary** (line 42) _____

❑ 8. **commitment** (line 45) _____

❑ 9. **exemplify** (line 54) _____

❑ 10. **dependable** (line 60) _____

Self-Tests

MyReadingLab Visit Chapter 2: Relationships in MyReadingLab to complete the Self-Test activities.

1 In each group, there are three synonyms and one antonym. Circle the antonym.

1. random	arbitrary	logical	impulsive
2. submissive	passive	obedient	aggressive
3. dedication	apathy	loyalty	commitment
4. represent	model	distort	exemplify
5. confusion	peacefulness	tranquility	serenity
6. compromise	cooperate	confront	bargain
7. release	control	hold	restrain
8. suggest	imply	hint	state
9. careless	trustworthy	dependable	responsible
10. pleasant	amiable	mean	agreeable

2 Finish the story using the vocabulary words. Use each word once.

VOCABULARY LIST

exemplify	serenity	arbitrary	compromise	commitment
amiable	restrain	dependable	imply	submissive

My (1)_____ at work was destroyed when I was asked to share my office with
a new coworker. I was chosen because I am considered an especially (2)_____
employee who gets the job done and works well with others. My supervisor has said that I
(3)_____ the type of person he likes to hire. When Hal arrived my happy world
was destroyed. Hal presented several problems, including his making (4)_____
decisions about our shared space. One day I came in and he had rearranged the furniture without
asking my opinion. Another day, I discovered that he had thrown out several of my files. I had made
a (5)_____ to myself to give Hal a month to adjust. However, after two weeks I had
to (6)_____ myself from yelling at him when he spent the entire day singing the
same song over and over. The next day, I walked in on Hal packing loads of company supplies
into a suitcase. He winked at me and asked me to keep this our secret. I told him I would not
(7)_____ my moral standards for him. After I told my supervisor what I had seen, Hal
had the nerve to (8)_____ that he had seen me doing something illegal. Despite my
being a good-natured individual, even the most (9)_____ person has a limit and this
was mine. I told my boss that I would no longer be (10)_____ and that either Hal or
I would be leaving the company that day. Goodbye, Hal!

3 Answer the following questions using the vocabulary words. Use each word once.

VOCABULARY LIST

submissive	serenity	commitment	compromise	exemplify
restraining	arbitrary	dependable	amiable	implies

1. If you agree to pick a friend up at the airport at 6 a.m., what have you made? _____

2. When you raise your eyebrows and say, "Oh, she's not going straight home," what does your comment do? _____

3. If you agree to everything your friends want to do even if it isn't really what you want to do, what are you being? _____

4. When the police put up a barricade so the crowd can't get too close to celebrities, what are they doing to the fans? _____

5. If you are fun to be around, how might people describe you? _____

6. What kind of feeling might you experience while spending a weekend at a cabin in the woods?

_____

7. When you tell a friend that you are willing to clean the dishes if he will cook, what are you offering? _____

8. If you are never late and you never forget an appointment, what kind of person are you? _____

9. When a member of your carpool suddenly announces that everyone needs to be at the meeting place a half hour earlier, what kind of decision has been made? _____

10. If you are quiet at the theater in the hope that your younger brother and sister will be, too, what are you trying to do? _____

Word Visions

Identify the two vocabulary words represented in the drawings.

1. _____

2. _____

Word Wise

Collocations

The salesman *gave his assurance* that the table would be delivered by Friday, so I would have it for my dinner party on Saturday. (Chapter 1) (Note: The collocation can also be *gave her assurance*.)

To *implement a plan* that will help you achieve your goals, begin by deciding which three goals are the most important. (Chapter 1)

My boss made an *arbitrary decision* that all employees would wear shorts on Fridays. Needless to say not everyone was happy with the idea. (Chapter 2)

Naya made a *commitment to* spend three hours a week volunteering at the local food bank. (Chapter 2)

Connotations and Denotations

Zealous (Chapter 1): denotation—"enthusiastic, eager; passionate." Many people see being zealous about an activity or interest as a positive emotion. For some people, however, the connotation of zealous conjures a person who has thrown oneself into an activity beyond the normal bounds of enthusiasm, making one a fanatic or zealot (an excessively zealous person).

Compromise (Chapter 2): one denotation as a verb—"to arrive at a settlement by yielding on certain points." Some people's connotation of compromise is to see it as a situation where both sides lose by giving away items that are important to them. Do you view a compromise as a form of bargaining where both parties win or lose?

Interactive Exercise

Take a few minutes to complete the following questions on getting along with people.

1. To achieve serenity with friends or family, what is something you need to make a commitment to do?

   _____

2. What trait of a good friend does one of your friends exemplify? Give an example of a time your friend displayed this trait.

   _____

   _____

   _____

3. What type of compromise have you made to preserve a relationship?

   _____

   _____

4. What kind of arbitrary decision could ruin a relationship?

   _____

5. What should people never imply if they want to maintain healthy relationships? What is a way to restrain oneself from making a statement that could hurt a friendship?

   _____

   _____

   _____

6. What qualities are important in a good friend? A good friend is... (Mark all that apply.)

   _____ dependable   _____ apathetic   _____ assured   _____ submissive

   _____ zealous   _____ amiable   _____ arbitrary   _____ attractive

HINT

Shades of Meaning

Learning new vocabulary is more than learning synonyms. While some words you learn may be similar to other words you know and may be used in place of another word, every word is unique. Good writers choose their words carefully. Words have different shades of meaning, and conscientious writers think about those differences when picking a word to use. A careful reader also responds to those differences in meaning. In some cases the differences are slight, such as "On Sundays I eat a big dinner" or "On Sundays I eat a large dinner." But replacing "big" or "large" with "huge" or "gigantic" (both synonyms for "big") does alter the image of how much food the person is eating. Some synonyms have even bigger differences. For the sentence, "The clever woman found a way to get out of debt," "clever" could be replaced with the synonyms "smart" or "crafty." The reader would have a different reaction to the woman depending on whether the writer selected "smart" or "crafty." When reading or writing, pay attention to the diverse ways words can be used.

Word List

amiable
[ā′ mē ə bəl]
adj. good-natured; agreeable

arbitrary
[är′ bi trer′ ē]
adj. 1. determined by chance or impulse, not by need or reason; random
2. based on individual judgment or preference

commitment
[kə mit′ mənt]
n. 1. a pledge to do something; a promise
2. the state of being devoted to a belief, a person, or course of action; loyalty

compromise
[kom′ prə mīz′]
v. 1. to arrive at a settlement by yielding on certain points; to cooperate; to bargain
2. to lower or weaken, such as standards
n. a settlement of differences where each side yields on certain points; a deal

dependable
[di pen′ də bəl]
adj. trustworthy; responsible

exemplify
[eg zem′ plə fī′, ig-]
v. to show by example; to model; to represent

imply
[im plī′]
v. to state indirectly; to suggest; to hint

restrain
[ri strān′]
v. to hold back or control; to prevent from doing something

serenity
[si ren′ ə tē]
n. peacefulness, tranquility

submissive
[səb mis′ iv]
adj. obedient; passive

Words to Watch

Which words would you like to practice with a bit more? Pick 3–5 words to study, and list them below. Write the word and its definition, and compose your own sentence using the word correctly. This extra practice could be the final touch to learning a word.

Word	Definition	Your Sentence
1. _____	_____	_____
	_____	_____
2. _____	_____	_____
	_____	_____
3. _____	_____	_____
	_____	_____
4. _____	_____	_____
	_____	_____
5. _____	_____	_____
	_____	_____

Chapter 3

Entertainment

Enjoying a Night Out

ENTERTAINMENT

Movie Sends Viewers to New Places

Planet Desire, rated PG-13, now playing at The Strand, Horizon, and Multiplex 11

Don't miss *Planet Desire*, a new action thriller,
5 showing in 3D. A shy, amiable young man is
drawn into a video game thanks to a computer
glitch. His sister discovers the malfunction and
sets out to save him despite her **aversion** to
technology. Breaking **protocol**, she arranges a
10 late-night **clandestine** meeting in an alley with
a computer genius who works for a secret
government agency. The genius agrees to help by
allowing her to play a **virtual** reality game he has
created. He gives her his assurance that the game
15 is safe and that it will connect her to her brother.
Her only hope is to step into the unknown, but can
she trust this man? The plot might sound wild, but
it feels real. You are right in the action during
the exciting 3D scenes of the siblings' adventures,
20 which include rafting, mountain climbing, and
scuba diving. The superb acting and soundtrack
also contribute to making this a must-see movie.

New Burger Place Serves Up Fun

Take a break from your **frenzied** studies and
head over to Pearl's for food and fun. Pearl's is a 25
great new burger place that is quickly becoming
popular with students. The menu features the
omnipresent hamburger, but Pearl's offers a few
unusual toppings. Some of the choices that may 30
intrigue you include blue cheese and gorgonzola
(cheddar and jack cheese are also available),
pineapple slices, jicama, and ice cream (yes, you
can have a dessert hamburger—it even comes
with a cherry on top). The menu also features 35
delicious fries, onion rings, Buffalo wings, and a
variety of salads and sandwiches. Desserts include
scrumptious pies and cakes. Pearl's has ten flavors
of shakes. I give a standing **ovation** to the banana
shake: it's the best shake I've ever tasted! Owner 40
Pearl Barnes is a **resourceful** woman. She has
managed to fit twenty tables and ten counter seats
into the small space, but the way she arranged
everything, the place doesn't feel crowded, even
on a busy Saturday night. Come enjoy good food 45
and fun people at Pearl's.

Located at 1543 Central Street, open for lunch
and dinner; low prices.

Predicting

For each set, write the definition on the line next to the word to which it belongs. If you are unsure, return to the reading, and underline any context clues you find. After you've made your predictions, check your answers against the Word List at the end of the chapter. Place a checkmark in the box next to each word whose definition you missed. These are the words you'll want to study closely.

Set One

simulated	a technical error	a strong dislike	private
a code of correct behavior			

☐ 1. **glitch** (line 7) _____

☐ 2. **aversion** (line 8) _____

☐ 3. **protocol** (line 9) _____

☐ 4. **clandestine** (line 10) _____

☐ 5. **virtual** (line 13) _____

Set Two

wild	present everywhere at once	approval	inventive	to fascinate

☐ 6. **frenzied** (line 25) _____

☐ 7. **omnipresent** (line 29) _____

☐ 8. **intrigue** (line 31) _____

☐ 9. **ovation** (line 39) _____

☐ 10. **resourceful** (line 41) _____

Self-Tests

MyReadingLab Visit Chapter 3: Entertainment in MyReadingLab to complete the Self-Test activities.

1 Match each term with its synonym in Set One and its antonym in Set Two.

Synonyms

Set One

_____ 1. glitch   a. private

_____ 2. intrigue   b. malfunction

_____ 3. omnipresent   c. etiquette

_____ 4. clandestine   d. plot

_____ 5. protocol   e. everywhere

Antonyms

Set Two

_____	6. aversion	f. unimaginative
_____	7. virtual	g. disapproval
_____	8. resourceful	h. actual
_____	9. frenzied	i. liking
_____	10. ovation	j. calm

2 Complete the sentences using the vocabulary words. Use each word once.

VOCABULARY LIST

virtual	intrigue	clandestine	glitch	frenzied
ovation	omnipresent	aversion	resourceful	protocol

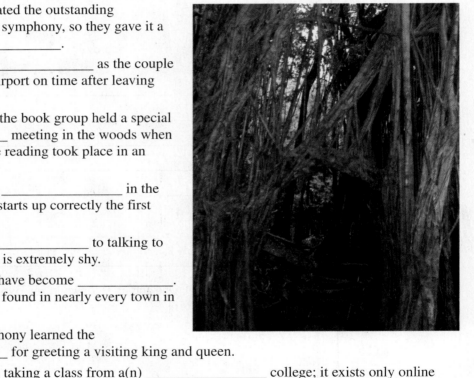

1. The crowd appreciated the outstanding performance of the symphony, so they gave it a standing _____.

2. The drive was _____ as the couple tried to get to the airport on time after leaving late.

3. Select members of the book group held a special _____ meeting in the woods when the novel they were reading took place in an enchanted forest.

4. There must be a(n) _____ in the computer; it never starts up correctly the first time.

5. Fran has a(n) _____ to talking to people because she is extremely shy.

6. Hamburger chains have become _____. At least one can be found in nearly every town in America.

7. As a diplomat, Anthony learned the _____ for greeting a visiting king and queen.

8. Next semester I am taking a class from a(n) _____ college; it exists only online without any real buildings.

9. There was a lot of _____ at work last month as people tried to figure out who was going to become the new president of the company.

10. Milton is _____. I have seen him fix a car with chewing gum and a paper clip when we were stranded on the side of the road.

3 Fill in each blank with the letter of the most logical analogy. See Completing Analogies on page 6 for instructions and practice.

Set One

1. romance : clandestine :: _____
2. frenzied : peaceful :: _____
3. a technical problem : glitch :: _____
4. great musician : ovation :: _____
5. plot of a novel : intrigue :: _____

a. an excellent student : an "A"
b. sofa : couch
c. departing friend : sadden
d. sleepy : awake
e. a garden : overgrown

Set Two

6. doctor : protocol :: _____
7. omnipresent : limited :: _____
8. computer games : virtual :: _____
9. aversion : snakes :: _____
10. resourceful : capable :: _____

f. fondness : cookies
g. beautiful : lovely
h. soldier : orders
i. jokes : funny
j. bitter : sweet

Word Wise

Collocations

Despite a *glitch in the system* at the beginning of the program that caused the stage to go black for ten minutes, the symphony still received a *standing ovation* at the end of the show. Every note had thrilled the crowd. (Chapter 3)

We may quite soon find *virtual reality* games in every home. We can play a game and really feel as if we are driving a racecar or diving underwater. (Chapter 3)

Interesting Etymologies

Glitch (Chapter 3) possibly comes from the Yiddish *glitsh*, meaning "a slip or slide," or from the German *glitshen,* meaning "to slip." The word was originally part of the technical language of American electronic engineers in the early 1960s. The word was popularized by the U.S. space program and went on to have a wider meaning than just dealing with electronic hardware.

Ovation (Chapter 3) comes from the Latin ōvatiō, meaning "rejoicing," which comes from *ovāre,* "to rejoice or exult." In Roman times, an ovation was a ceremonial entrance of a commander into Rome whose military victories, while important and worth celebrating, were not of the degree that warranted a triumph.

Interactive Version: Envision yourself as a restaurant reviewer, and write a short review using either photograph as your inspiration. You can write about a real restaurant you enjoy going to or create an imaginary one. Use at least five of the vocabulary words in your review.

_____

_____

_____

_____

_____

_____

_____

_____

_____

_____

_____

_____

_____

_____

_____

Conversation Starters

An excellent way to review the vocabulary words and help to make them your own is to use them when you are speaking. Gather three to five friends or classmates, and use one or more of the conversation starters below. Before you begin talking, have each person write down six of the vocabulary words he or she will use during the conversation. Share your lists with each other to check that you did not all pick the same six words. Try to cover all of the words you want to study, whether you are reviewing one, two, or more chapters.

1. What advice on study skills would you give to a student entering college?
2. How do you resolve conflicts with family, friends, or coworkers?
3. Where do you go to enjoy a night out? What has made an evening especially entertaining?
4. What can students do to find a balance between studying, meeting commitments to family and friends, and participating in fun activities?

Word List

aversion
[ə vûr′ zhən, -shən]

n. 1. a strong dislike of something and a desire to avoid it; hatred
2. a cause or object of such a dislike

clandestine
[klan des′ tin]

adj. secret; private

frenzied
[fren′ zēd]

adj. wild; agitated; mad

glitch
[glich]

n. a minor malfunction or technical error

intrigue
[in′ trēg, in trēg′]

v. to fascinate
n. a scheme; a plot

omnipresent
[om′ ni prez′ ənt]

adj. present everywhere at once

ovation
[ō vā′ shən]

n. applause; approval

protocol
[prō′ tə kol′]

n. 1. a code of correct behavior; the etiquette diplomats follow
2. a plan for a medical treatment or scientific experiment

resourceful
[ri sôrs′ fəl]

adj. able to deal skillfully with new situations; capable; inventive

virtual
[vûr′ choo əl]

adj. 1. created or run by a computer; simulated
2. almost existing; near

Words to Watch

Which words would you like to practice with a bit more? Pick 3–5 words to study, and list them below. Write the word and its definition, and compose your own sentence using the word correctly. This extra practice could be the final touch to learning a word.

Word	Definition	Your Sentence
1. _____	_____	_____
_____	_____	_____
2. _____	_____	_____
_____	_____	_____
3. _____	_____	_____
_____	_____	_____
4. _____	_____	_____
_____	_____	_____
5. _____	_____	_____
_____	_____	_____

Chapter 4

Word Parts I

Look for words with these **prefixes**, **roots**, and/or **suffixes** as you work through this book. You may have already seen some of them, and you will see others in later chapters. Learning basic word parts can help you figure out the meanings of unfamiliar words.

prefix: a word part added to the beginning of a word that changes the meaning of the root

root: a word's basic part with its essential meaning

suffix: a word part added to the end of a word; indicates the part of speech

Word Part	Meaning	Examples and Definitions
Prefixes		
am-	love	*amorous:* being in love *amateur:* a person who does something for the love of it without getting paid
eu-	good, well	*euphoria:* a feeling of extreme well-being *eulogy:* a speech that says good things about a person
omni-	all	*omnipresent:* present at all places *omniscient:* knowing all
Roots		
-cis-	cut	*precise:* accurate; to the point; cut short *incisive:* cutting; penetrating
-cla-, -clo-, -clu-	shut, close	*claustrophobia:* a fear of enclosed places *conclude:* to shut or close
-fin-	end, limit	*finalist:* a person allowed to compete at the end of a contest *finite:* having an end or limit
-mis-, -mit-	send	*emissary:* a person sent on a mission *transmit:* to send across
-ple-	fill	*implement:* to apply so as to ensure the fulfillment of *supplement:* to fill in for a shortage
Suffixes		
-ary (makes an adjective)	pertaining to or connected with	*arbitrary:* connected with the power to judge *sedentary:* pertaining to inactivity
-ify, -fy (makes a verb)	to make	*exemplify:* to make an example of *clarify:* to make clear

1 Read each definition, and choose the appropriate word from the list below. Use each word once. The meaning of the word part is underlined to help you make the connection. Refer to the Word Parts list if you need help.

VOCABULARY LIST

ordinary	concise	complement	infinite	eulogy
amorously	dismiss	omnipotent	magnify	exclude

1. in a manner filled with <u>love</u> _____
2. to <u>send</u> away _____
3. <u>pertaining to</u> the everyday _____
4. brief, <u>cut</u> short _____
5. to <u>shut</u> others out _____
6. <u>to make</u> bigger _____
7. to <u>fill</u> out or make whole _____
8. a speech about a person's <u>good</u> qualities, usually given after a person dies _____
9. <u>end</u>less _____
10. <u>all</u> powerful _____

2 Finish the sentences with the meaning of each word part. Use each meaning once. The word part is underlined to help you make the connection.

VOCABULARY LIST

all	love	fill	send	connected with
cut	end	shut	to make	good

1. My boyfriend used the <u>eu</u>phemistic phrase "exploring options" to explain why we should break up; he wanted it to sound like a(n) _____ thing.
2. A de<u>fin</u>itive answer would put a(n) _____ to a question.
3. When the bank fore<u>clos</u>ed on the business, its doors were _____ forever.
4. An <u>am</u>ateur plays a sport for the _____ of it.
5. S<u>ciss</u>ors are used to _____ paper.
6. The <u>omni</u>scient narrator in the novel knew what was happening to _____ the characters.
7. The lover had to _____ a <u>miss</u>ive right away asking forgiveness for that morning's fight.
8. To com<u>ple</u>te the form, you need to _____ in all of the information about your past medical treatments.
9. When you clar<u>ify</u> something, you aim _____ it easier to understand.
10. My dad made the arbit<u>rary</u> decision that I should be home from dates by nine because he feels he has the right to make judgments about anything _____ his daughter.

3 Finish the story using the word parts. Use each word part once. Your knowledge of word parts, as well as the context clues, will help you create the correct words. If you do not understand the meaning of a word you have made, check your dictionary for the definition or to see whether the word exists.

WORD PARTS

eu	clu	ple	ary	cis
fin	ify	mit	am	omni

An Adventure

I am usually a sedent(1)_____
person, but a friend of mine convinced me to
take a combination hiking and camel-trekking
trip with her. Due to various circumstances,
the time seemed right to try something
new. It was near my thirtieth birthday,
and signs of my growing older seemed
(2)_____present, so I figured
"why not." I was also looking for
se(3)_____sion and peace in a
natural setting away from my big-city life.

    I thought I might have to ver(4)_____ my sanity when I first saw the line of camels
approaching. I was going to ride one of those? The first day, however, was great. The guide was very
(5)_____iable, and he said I was riding like I had been doing it since I was born. I was
possibly getting a little too confident. My (6)_____phoria disappeared near the end
of day three when I fell off my camel with a big thud. I skinned my left knee and elbow. Luckily, I
wasn't hurt worse. The guide cleaned my wounds and tried to assure me that I would be fine.

    I wasn't feeling confident about continuing the next day, but our guide had an idea. He grabbed
a knife to im(7)_____ment his plan, which scared me for a minute. However, he used
it to make two small in(8)_____ions in my saddle and wrapped a piece of rope through
them to make a seatbelt for me. He said I could use it until I got my confidence back. My friend said
she would also be trans(9)_____ting positive thoughts to me. She must have sent a lot of
good feelings my way because by the afternoon I undid my seatbelt. The rest of the trip was wonderful! I'm de(10)_____itely going to spend the rest of my life having more adventures and
seeing new places.

4 Pick the best definition for each underlined word using your knowledge of word parts. Circle the word part in each of the underlined words.

a. cutting; penetrating

b. to make invalid

c. to limit

d. eating all kinds of food

e. a good or painless death

f. filled with love

g. excess; filled with more than enough

h. a person closed off from others

i. connected with using as a backup

j. sending or happening irregularly

_____ 1. My cousin is a <u>recluse</u> who lives in the woods and only goes to town twice a year.

_____ 2. <u>Euthanasia</u> is a controversial subject; it can be hard to decide when to end a life.

_____ 3. The lawyer's questions were so <u>incisive</u> that the defendant was unable to hide what happened at the murder scene.

_____ 4. <u>Omnivorous</u> eaters can satisfy their hunger with plants or animals.

_____ 5. Yasmin's <u>intermittent</u> letters left us wondering what she was doing in the months she didn't write us.

_____ 6. My teacher said to <u>confine</u> my research paper to eight pages.

_____ 7. As soon as she saw the puppy, the little girl hugged it and became <u>enamored</u> of it.

_____ 8. After my mother died, my father decided to <u>nullify</u> his will and create a new one naming his children as his beneficiaries.

_____ 9. Once the trunk was bursting, I assured my wife that is was time to leave the mall as we had a <u>plethora</u> of gifts for two children.

_____ 10. When the power went out, the hospital employed its <u>auxiliary</u> generator.

5 A good way to remember word parts is to pick one word that uses a word part and understand how that word part functions in the word. Then you can apply that meaning to other words that have the same word part. Use the following words to help you match the word part to its meaning.

Set One

_____ 1. **am-:** amorous, amiable, amateur

_____ 2. **-ple-:** implement, complement, complete

_____ 3. **eu-:** euphoria, euphemism, eulogy

_____ 4. **-mis-, -mit-:** emissary, transmit, intermittent

_____ 5. **-ary:** arbitrary, emissary, sedentary

a. fill

b. send

c. love

d. good, well

e. pertaining to or connected with

Set Two

_____ 6. **-fin-:** finalist, finite, confine

_____ 7. **omni-:** omniscient, omnipresent, omnipotent

_____ 8. **-cis-:** incisive, concise, scissors

_____ 9. **-cla-, -clo-, -clu-:** claustrophobia, enclose, seclude

_____ 10. **-ify, -fy:** exemplify, rectify, satisfy

f. to make

g. cut

h. end, limit

i. all

j. shut, close

Interactive Exercise

Use the dictionary to find a word you don't know that uses each word part listed below. Write the meaning of the word part, the word, and the definition. If your dictionary has the etymology (history) of the word, see how the word part relates to the meaning, and write the etymology after the definition.

Word Part	Meaning	Word	Definition and Etymology
EXAMPLE:			
–fin–	end, limit	finial	a small ending ornament at the top of a gable, arch, spire, or other object
			Latin "finis," meaning end
1. am–			
2. eu–			
3. omni–			
4. -clo-			
5. -fin-			

HINT

Etymologies

An etymology is the history of a word. Some dictionaries, usually at the end of an entry, will tell how the word came into existence. There are several ways words are developed, such as being made up, coming from a person's name, or evolving over time from foreign languages. Reading a word's etymology can sometimes help you remember the meaning. For example, the word **addict** comes from the Latin *addictus*, which meant someone given to another as a slave. This history helps to show how being addicted to something is being a slave to it. Not all words have interesting histories, but taking the time to read an etymology can be useful. If you get excited about word origins, there are books available on the subject that show how fascinating words can be.

Match each photograph to one of the word parts below, and write the meaning of the word part.

am-   -cis-   -cla-/-clo-/-clu-   -ple-   -ary

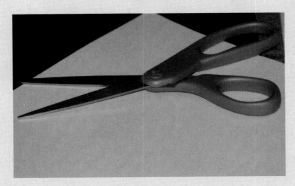

1. _____

2. _____

Word Wise

Internet Activity: Creating a Blog

You can use the Internet to develop your vocabulary by writing e-mails to classmates or friends that contain the vocabulary words or get several class members to agree on a time to access the Internet and instant message each other to feel like you are using the words in a conversation. You can also explore the world of Web logs, or blogs for short.

A blog is an online journal, and they have become increasingly popular in recent years. With a blog you can express your thoughts on whatever interests you: sports, politics, music. Other people on the Web can read your blog, make comments back to you, and link your site to theirs. A blog gives you a chance to express your opinions, share your creative writing, or find others with similar interests. You can also add photographs and create links to Web sites you enjoy.

Starting a blog is easy. Try blogger.com or LiveJournal.com to get started; both are free services. You can also search the Web for other blog services. It is possible to create a group blog, so several classmates or the whole class can be involved. Just go through the steps listed on a site, and you can be blogging in five minutes. Make a conscious effort to use the week's vocabulary words in your blog. To make comments to each other, again using the vocabulary words, get the addresses of at least two other students' blogs.

Remember to be careful about the personal information you share on the Web. You can create a profile of yourself on your blog. Avoid giving out information such as your address and phone number and, of course, passwords. You may want to create a new e-mail address to use when you set up your blog. See Chapter 13 for information on Internet scams. Enjoy the ability to communicate with a wide audience, but be alert for those who want to abuse the power of the Internet.

Review

Focus on Chapters 1–4

The following activities give you the opportunity to further interact with the vocabulary words you've been learning. By taking tests, answering questions, using visuals, doing a crossword puzzle, and working with others, you will see which words you know well and which ones need additional study.

Self-Tests MyReadingLab Visit Chapter 5: Review in MyReadingLab to complete the Self-Test activities.

LO 4, 8 1 Match each term with its synonym in Set One and its antonym in Set Two.

Synonyms

Set One

_____	1. enable	a. capable
_____	2. virtual	b. boredom
_____	3. resourceful	c. simulated
_____	4. compromise	d. bargain
_____	5. apathy	e. permit

Antonyms

Set Two

_____	6. serenity	f. calm
_____	7. intermittent	g. free
_____	8. frenzied	h. conceal
_____	9. indicate	i. disorder
_____	10. restrain	j. steady

After completing the Review chapter activities, turn to Word Reactions on page 175, and add your first set of words to the lists.

2 Pick the word that best completes each sentence.

1. I wasn't sure of company _____, so I called my manager to find out if I could take a client to lunch.

   a. ovation   b. serenity   c. protocol   d. terminology

2. I didn't mean to _____ that Jayden was lazy when I said I was amazed that he was still in his panamas at noon, but I was surprised that he wasn't dressed yet.

   a. imply   b. intrigue   c. compromise   d. undermine

3. I need to stop _____ myself when I do poorly on a test and start studying more.

   a. intriguing   b. exemplifying   c. indicating   d. berating

4. Tony is such a(n) _____ worker that he had the house half painted by the time the other volunteers arrived.

   a. virtual   b. arbitrary   c. clandestine   d. zealous

5. With all the whispering in the halls, there is obviously some _____ going on at work.

   a. intrigue   b. serenity   c. glitch   d. assurance

6. The _____ in an art history class can be challenging to learn. There are so many words one can use to describe a painting.

   a. serenity   b. terminology   c. ovation   d. commitment

7. Rosa is determined to no longer _____ her success by thinking negative thoughts. From now on she will have a can-do attitude.

   a. undermine   b. exemplify   c. intrigue   d. enable

8. I was tired of the _____ meetings with my new girlfriend. I told her that we needed to quit meeting secretly or break up.

   a. intermittent   b. amiable   c. clandestine   d. omnipresent

3 Pick the vocabulary word that best completes the sentence. Use each word once.

zealous	amiable	virtual	submissive	omnipresent

1. Malila is usually a pleasant person, but she wasn't that _____ at the party last night. I wonder if something is wrong with her.

2. I vowed to no longer be _____, so I told my boss it was time for the raise he had been promising or I was gone. He gave me the raise.

3. Food seemed to be _____ at the party, or maybe it just felt that way because I was on a diet.

4. The woman was _____ about running; she went out even when two feet of snow covered the ground.

5. The _____ office program shows that our company could be more efficient if we rearrange our work spaces.

LO 4 **4** Complete the following sentences that illustrate collocations. The rest of the collocation is in italics. Use each word or phrase once.

a plan	in the system	to	gave his	standing
reality	decision			

1. The audience was so impressed with the violinist's skills that it gave her a _____ *ovation.*

2. Due to a *glitch* _____, your credit card was billed twice for your meal. I was able to fix the problem.

3. For more than three miles my family couldn't decide what type of food they wanted, so I made the *arbitrary* _____ to stop at the next restaurant we drove by.

4. It has taken hard work by several individuals to *implement* _____ as big as this one.

5. On her wedding day, Antonia made a *commitment* _____ honor and cherish her husband.

6. The president of the company _____ *assurance* that the plant would not close and send jobs overseas.

7. One of the benefits of *virtual* _____ programs is that they can help us learn how to adapt to different environments.

LO 5 **5** Fill in the missing word part, and circle the meaning of the word part found in each sentence.

Example: Jess built an en*clo*sure to (shut) in the hens.

omni	ple	mis	ary	am	ify

1. The suspect's recent purchases looked arbitr_____, but the police felt that they were somehow connected with a larger plan.

2. It will be difficult to im_____ment Dan's plan because we need to fill three vacant positions before it can work.

3. To make my parents and brothers proud of me, I try hard to exempl_____ a good student.

4. Campaign signs are _____present in my town months before an election; they are all over the place.

5. Yoki is so sub_____sive that I could send her to the grocery ten times in one day and she wouldn't complain.

6. I love being around Katy because she is such a(n) _____iable person who always cheers me up.

Answers to the analogies exercise in the Getting Started section on page 7:

1. d   2. a   3. b   4. c   5. thaw   6. joy   7. geese   8. spice

---

6 Finish the story using the vocabulary words below. Use each word once.

VOCABULARY LIST

apathy	aversion	commitment	dependable	enable
exemplified	frenzied	resourceful	submissive	undermine

Appreciating Nature

I used to have a(n) (1)_____ to sleeping
on the ground. And at best I had (2)_____
toward carrying a pack on my back, but when I
dropped off friends for an overnight hike at Hidden
Glen, I was intrigued by the beauty at the start of the
hike. My friend said the lovely wooded pathway
(3)_____ the rest of the area. He told
me about forests to explore, meadows to wander in,
and streams to camp near. He also said I was too
much of a wimp to ever join them. I decided then that
I wouldn't let his comments (4)_____
my desire to see what was beyond the path.

 The next day I went out shopping for a backpack. The clerk recommended one that would
(5)_____ me to carry my essential gear
and still be lightweight. He also helped me pick out other equipment that he said every
(6)_____ hiker should have. Two weeks later, after a(n) (7)_____ night
of packing and repacking, I was ready the next morning when my friends picked me up. On that first
hike I was pretty (8)_____ and did whatever my friends told me. Now, after five years of
backpacking, I have become a(n) (9)_____ leader who can be trusted to make important
decisions. I have made a real (10)_____ to protecting and enjoying the natural world.

Interactive Exercise

LO 2 Answer the following questions to further test your understanding of the vocabulary words.

1. What are two signs that would indicate a person is interested in meeting you?

    _____

2. What are two situations or items that people should not compromise on?

    _____

3. Where would you hold a clandestine meeting in your town? Why is it a good place for such a meeting?

    _____

4. Name two courses where you have had to learn new terminology.

    _____

5. What are two techniques you use to restrain your anger when someone is annoying you?

    _____

6. What would you do if there was a glitch in your computer system the night before you had a paper due?

    _____

7. What are two activities that you do intermittently?

    _____

8. What do you do to restore your serenity after a busy week?

    _____

9. What is something you have an aversion to? Why do you think you feel this way?

    _____

10. What does a performer need to do to get a standing ovation from you?

    _____

HINT

Make Your Own Tests

A great way to study is to make your own tests in the same style of the tests that you will have in class. Making the tests puts you in the instructor's frame of mind and makes you think about what is important to study.

- Before the first test (or quiz), ask your instructor what format(s) the test will be in—true/false, multiple choice, matching, essay.
- Create a test in the same format(s) with questions that you think will be asked, neatly handwritten or typed. Set the test aside for a day.
- The next day, take the test and correct yourself. How much did you remember?
- Make a test for a friend, and exchange tests with each other. Did you come up with similar questions?
- If you examine the first in-class test, you will have a better idea of what the instructor is looking for, and then your homemade tests will be even more useful.

LO 3,6

Name It

Write three titles or headlines for each photograph.
Use at least six of the words below in your titles or
headlines. Feel free to add word endings (i.e., -s, -ing, -ly). It might help you to imagine the photograph as hanging in an art gallery, on the cover of a book, or accompanying an article in a newspaper or magazine. Your titles/headlines can be serious or humorous. Share what you have written with your classmates. Your instructor may ask the class to vote on the titles and headlines that best capture the mood or action of each photograph.

EXAMPLES

Title: **Serenity** in a Soda

Headline: **Resourceful** Parents Know When to
Give Kids a Shopping Break

VOCABULARY LIST

assurance	enable	arbitrary
intermittent	berate	serenity
dependable	imply	aversion
implement	protocol	frenzied
resourceful	intrigue	commitment

1. _____

_____

2. _____

_____

3. _____

_____

1. _____

_____

2. _____

_____

3. _____

_____

Crossword Puzzle

LO 3

Across

1. a deal
3. "I'm eager to get started!"
4. the opposite of submit
7. trustworthy; responsible
11. a minor technical error
13. Diplomats need to learn this.
14. to hint
16. ten children in a small house, for example
18. Eating hamburgers and fries daily may do this to one's health.
19. almost existing
20. self-confidence or a promise

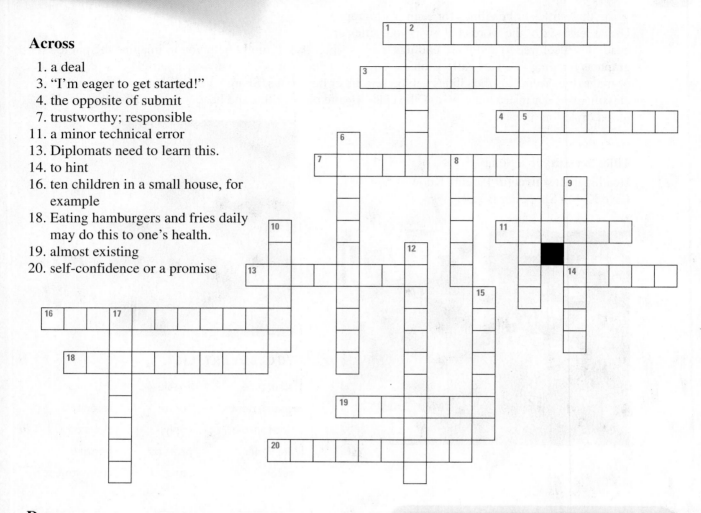

Down

2. "Bravo!" and "Encore!" along with clapping
5. to model or represent
6. arrhythmia, ketosis, aneurysm, as examples
8. "Whatever."
9. James Bond is always involved in this.
10. "You never do anything right!"
12. for example, a meeting in a dark alley
15. "Sounds fun—I'd love to try Greek food."
17. to be a sign of

Use the following words to complete the crossword puzzle. Use each word once.

VOCABULARY LIST

amiable	indicate
apathy	intrigue
assurance	omnipresent
berate	ovation
clandestine	protocol
compromise	restrain
dependable	terminology
exemplify	undermine
glitch	virtual
imply	zealous

Mix It Up LO 3,7,8

Matching Meanings

Get four to six classmates together, and make teams of two to three people. You will need two sets of flash cards. Lay out a rectangle of 25 flash cards with the words face up. Lay out another rectangle of the same 25 words with the definitions face up. (You can make larger or smaller rectangles, but it is best to have at least fifteen words, and no more than forty.) One person on a team picks up a word and tries to find the matching definition in the other rectangle. Teammates can help the person. If the person is right, he or she gets to keep both cards. If the person is wrong, he or she returns the cards to their places. A team can keep going until it misses a match. When all the words and definitions are matched, the team with the most cards wins. This activity can also be played with pairs, or you can test yourself individually if you have two sets of flash cards (or you can write the words on slips of paper and match them to the definition side of your flash cards).

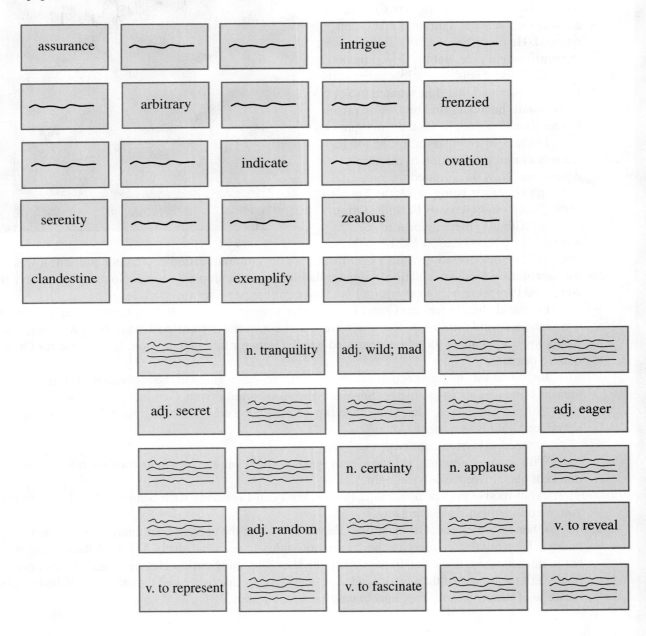

Chapter 6

Science Fiction

The Silent Stars

They had lost contact with the Earth. The crew didn't know this yet, but they would soon. They had been sent to **subjugate** the newly discovered life on Jupiter. Conquering
5 another race was not a mission that Orion enjoyed. He never believed that humans were the **omnipotent** race, but the government felt otherwise, and it was impossible to resist its force. He was told that if he wanted to voice
10 any **dissent**, he would find himself in prison. Rather than disagree, he took the assignment.

His lack of enthusiasm for the job had led to a **cursory** inspection of the ship's equipment. Now he regretted the rush,
15 although no longer being under the Earth's surveillance might have its benefits. Orion checked with his chief engineer to see whether the **precise** reason for the malfunction could be discovered. It wasn't a problem with the communication equipment after all; it was a
20 **miscalculation** by the navigation computer that had sent the ship off course. No one knew where they were, and they were no longer within range to communicate with any satellites.

He could already feel the Grand Commander's anger. When, or if, they returned, he was sure the commander would **annihilate** the whole crew. The commander's **antipathy** for those who failed was well known. He had all too often destroyed whole fleets for failing a mission. It was time for Orion to
25 make a decision.

Just as he was to announce to the crew that there was a glitch in the navigation system and that their mission was about to change, Sergeant Aurora escorted Private Gemini into the room.

"Sir, we discovered what caused the problem with the navigation computer. Private Gemini introduced a virus into the program."

30 Amazed, all Orion could ask was "Why?"

With absolute serenity, Private Gemini explained, "I can't go on another mission to take over an innocent planet. We haven't the right."

"Your motive may be honorable, Private, but I can't **condone** such behavior. I will have to put you in confinement. Take her away."

35 When he was alone, Orion smiled. He would release the clever and attractive private in a couple of days. He would soon interview her more thoroughly to see what she had done to the computer, but in his heart he felt she had helped them all. They were now **emissaries** for peace. It was time to finally tell the crew that they were headed on a mission of discovery and that they would be bringing a message of peace to those they encountered among the stars.

Predicting

For each set, write the definition on the line next to the word to which it belongs. If you are unsure, return to the reading, and underline any context clues you find. After you've made your predictions, check your answers against the Word List at the end of the chapter. Place a checkmark in the box next to each word whose definition you missed. These are the words you'll want to study closely.

Set One

having unlimited authority or power	exact	to differ in opinion	to conquer	hasty

☐ 1. **subjugate** (line 3) _____

☐ 2. **omnipotent** (line 7) _____

☐ 3. **dissent** (line 10) _____

☐ 4. **cursory** (line 13) _____

☐ 5. **precise** (line 18) _____

Set Two

to destroy	to forgive	a mistake in planning	dislike	representatives sent on a mission

☐ 6. **miscalculation** (line 20) _____

☐ 7. **annihilate** (line 23) _____

☐ 8. **antipathy** (line 23) _____

☐ 9. **condone** (line 33) _____

☐ 10. **emissaries** (line 37) _____

Self-Tests

> **MyReadingLab** Visit Chapter 6: Science Fiction in MyReadingLab to complete the Self-Test activities.

1 Circle the correct word to complete each sentence.

1. The dictator tried to (annihilate, subjugate) the people so they would work in the fields.

2. I realized I needed to do more than a (precise, cursory) proofreading of my papers after I got a "D" on my first essay.

3. Because of one little (antipathy, miscalculation), we ended up twenty miles from where we wanted to be.

4. I can't (dissent, condone) the newspaper's sloppy coverage of the city's plans for downtown redevelopment; it has not investigated how the changes are going to affect those who live downtown.

5. I didn't like it when Reina was my baby-sitter because she thought she was (cursory, omnipotent).

6. I wanted to (annihilate, condone) the crab grass; it was ruining an otherwise beautiful lawn.

7. I have an (antipathy, emissary) for spicy mustards on my sandwiches.

8. Since the two countries were at war, the (miscalculation, emissary) secretly met with the king to discuss plans to settle the dispute.

9. I am (precise, omnipotent) when I make an online order so I don't get the wrong items.

10. I had to (subjugate, dissent) when asked if I agreed with moving the meeting to Thursday; I already had plans for that day.

2 Match the quotation to the word it best illustrates. Context clues are underlined to help you. Use each word once.

Set One

> **VOCABULARY LIST**
>
> annihilate   antipathy   emissary   condone   miscalculation

1. "I <u>hate</u> shopping. How can some people spend all day at a mall?" _____

2. "<u>I will deliver your message</u> to the president when I meet with her next week after my return home." _____

3. "I thought if we left at three o'clock we would have plenty of time to make it by five. I forgot about the bridge construction delay. I <u>planned wrong</u>, again." _____

4. "I can <u>overlook</u> your coming home late this time since you helped your sick friend get home safely." _____

5. "We <u>destroyed</u> that team 63 to 0." _____

Set Two

> **VOCABULARY LIST**
>
> omnipotent   dissent   cursory   precise   subjugate

6. "You must be <u>accurate</u> when you take these pills: take the red pill at noon every day and the blue pill at 10 a.m. every other day." _____

7. "I have <u>conquered</u> your country—bow down before me!" _____

8. "I <u>looked the report over quickly</u>, Doris, and it seems fine." _____

9. "I <u>beg to differ</u> with the committee. I think the plan will work." _____

10. "As fire chief, the City Council has given me <u>full authority</u> to handle the spreading wild fires." _____

3 Use the vocabulary words to complete the following analogies. See Completing Analogies on page 6 for instructions and practice.

Set One

> **VOCABULARY LIST**
>
> cursory   dissent   annihilate   antipathy   emissary

1. grow : flowers :: _____ : weeds

2. friend : warmth :: enemy : _____

3. accept : reject :: _____ : careful

4. mother : scolding :: _____ : message

5. assent : agree :: _____ : differ

6. baker : cake :: tired person : _____

7. distant : close :: _____ : powerless

8. fortunate : lucky :: exact : _____

9. crown : a king :: _____ : a slave

10. rain : flowers :: special circumstances : _____

 # Word Wise

Context Clue Mini-Lesson 2

This lesson uses antonyms—words that mean the opposite of the unknown word—as the clues. In the paragraph below, circle the antonyms you find for the underlined words and then, on the lines that follow the paragraph, write a word that is opposite the antonym as your definition of the word.

The opening night of the new art exhibit didn't start well. I saw a man <u>grimace</u> as he studied a painting of bright yellow and orange flowers. What was wrong? Most people would smile at such a scene. I heard a woman swear behind me. I wondered what painting could have <u>incensed</u> her so; most of the works were meant to calm people. I was feeling <u>despondent.</u> Looking for a way to cheer myself up, I spied the refreshment table. The pastries I had ordered from the new bakery looked delicious. I took a bite and finally understood what was upsetting people. Instead of sugar, the bakery had put salt in the icing. I would not, however, let my guests <u>forsake</u> me because of a salty pastry. I threw the tray in the trash and sent my assistant to buy cookies. I persuaded those in attendance to remain with promises of special deals and more goodies to come.

Your Definition

1. Grimace _____

2. Incensed _____

3. Despondent _____

4. Forsake _____

Interactive Version: Use the artwork and sentence starters as inspiration to write a science fiction story. Use at least six of the vocabulary words in your story. Feel free to add word endings (i.e., -s, -ed) if needed.

1. When the spaceships arrived, _____
   _____
   _____

2. The public shortly learned _____
   _____
   _____

3. Most people were surprised _____
   _____

4. After a week, nations were still unsure _____
   _____

5. Ten months later, world leaders _____
   _____

6. Just before the spaceships departed, _____
   _____

Word Part Reminder

Below are a few exercises to help you review the word parts you have been learning. Fill in the missing word part from the list, and circle the meaning of the word part found in each sentence. Try to complete the questions without returning to the Word Parts chapter, but if you get stuck, look back at Chapter 4.

omni   cis   ple   fy

1. I wanted to make my stomach happy, and the only thing I felt that would satis_____ it was a slice of pizza.

2. I am excited to read the _____bus volume that just came out because it is a collection of all of the short stories by my favorite writer.

3. Before he began to cut material for a suit, my uncle would check his measurements three times. Because he was so pre_____e, he never made a mistake.

4. It will be difficult for me to fill my orders if you keep de_____ting my supply by eating the cookies as soon as they come out of the oven.

Word List

annihilate
[ə nī′ ə lāt′]

   v. to destroy; to defeat completely

antipathy
[an tip′ ə thē]

   n. an aversion; an opposition in feeling; dislike

condone
[kən dōn′]

   v. 1. to forgive or pardon; to excuse
   2. to overlook; to ignore something illegal or offensive; to give unstated approval to

cursory
[kûr′ sə rē]

   adj. going rapidly over something, without noticing details; hasty; superficial

dissent
[di sent′]

   v. to differ in feeling or opinion, especially from the majority

   n. a difference of opinion

emissary
[em′ ə ser′ ē]

   n. 1. a representative sent on a mission; a delegate
   2. an agent sent on a secret mission

miscalculation
[mis kal′ kyə lā′ shən]

   n. a mistake in planning or forecasting

omnipotent
[om nip′ ə tənt]

   adj. having great or unlimited authority or power

precise
[pri sīs′]

   adj. 1. exact; accurate; definite
   2. strictly correct; demanding

subjugate
[sub′ jə gāt′]

   v. to conquer; to master; to dominate

Words to Watch

Which words would you like to practice with a bit more? Pick 3–5 words to study, and list them below. Write the word and its definition, and compose your own sentence using the word correctly. This extra practice could be the final touch to learning a word.

Word	Definition	Your Sentence
1. _____	_____	_____
_____	_____	_____
2. _____	_____	_____
_____	_____	_____
3. _____	_____	_____
_____	_____	_____
4. _____	_____	_____
_____	_____	_____
5. _____	_____	_____
_____	_____	_____

Chapter 7

Romance

A Knock on the Door

Estella slowly unfastens the lock. It is one o'clock in the morning—who could possibly be knocking so rapidly? Little does she know the **pandemonium** that is going to disturb her quiet night. Her big brown eyes open wide when she sees
5 Byron's **virile** build fill the doorway. His manliness causes Estella's heart to pound as quickly as his knocking on the door. It has been five months since they broke up, but she is once again in an **amorous** mood after admiring Byron's strong frame.
"I must see you," he gasps.

10   The **provocative** look in his eyes is one Estella cannot resist. She motions him inside and shuts the door.

Byron stumbles to the couch and collapses. Estella spies the blood stain on Byron's chest. She tears off her robe and presses it against his rippling muscles, so easily noticeable under
15 the damp shirt. Byron's eyes slowly open. He smiles and draws her closer.

"Estella," he whispers, "I need your help. If you no longer **abhor** me, please, please, hide me."

Estella pulls away. She stares at Byron trying to penetrate his thoughts. Does he actually believe she hates him? Could he really not know how she feels?

20   Byron begins to open his mouth, but Estella puts her finger to his lips.

"Oh, Byron, I don't hate you. You know you have come to the perfect place for **seclusion**. Let's not **delude** ourselves any longer. We are the ideal team. We were fooling ourselves by thinking we could work or love better alone."

Estella's thoughts wander to the night in Istanbul when they barely escaped, and then a vision
25 of a foggy morning in Paris pretending to be tourists takes shape. That memory is pushed aside by images of an eventful evening in Hong Kong.

"Estella, where are you?"

Byron's voice brings her back to reality. "You must know that you are always safe with me," she sighs as she takes his hand.

30   "I love you, too, Estella. Unfortunately, there is no time to **embellish** my story, even though it is a good one. The simple truth is I am being chased by . . ."

Estella smiles and pulls Byron to her. **Oblivious** to the danger close by, they embrace. A pounding at the door soon shatters their **euphoria**.

"We know you're in there, Byron. Come out, or we'll break down the door!"

35   A quick look passes between the two of them. They know what they need to do.

Predicting

For each set, write the definition on the line next to the word to which it belongs. If you are unsure, return to the reading, and underline any context clues you find. After you've made your predictions, check your answers against the Word List at the end of the chapter. Place a checkmark in the box next to each word whose definition you missed. These are the words you'll want to study closely.

Set One

to hate	passionate	strong	chaos	exciting

❑ 1. **pandemonium** (line 3) _____

❑ 2. **virile** (line 5) _____

❑ 3. **amorous** (line 8) _____

❑ 4. **provocative** (line 10) _____

❑ 5. **abhor** (line 17) _____

Set Two

to add details	to fool	a feeling of extreme happiness	unaware	solitude

❑ 6. **seclusion** (line 21) _____

❑ 7. **delude** (line 22) _____

❑ 8. **embellish** (line 30) _____

❑ 9. **oblivious** (line 32) _____

❑ 10. **euphoria** (line 33) _____

Self-Tests

MyReadingLab Visit Chapter 7: Romance in MyReadingLab to complete the Self-Test activities.

1 In each group, there are three synonyms and one antonym. Circle the antonym.

1. unaware	oblivious	attentive	forgetful
2. provocative	boring	exciting	stimulating
3. manly	weak	strong	virile
4. adore	hate	abhor	detest
5. delude	trick	mislead	trust
6. joy	euphoria	sadness	jubilation
7. chaos	disorder	peace	pandemonium
8. isolation	exposure	solitude	seclusion
9. cold	amorous	loving	passionate
10. elaborate	exaggerate	embellish	minimize

2 Finish these sentences from a fictitious tabloid magazine. Use each word once.

VOCABULARY LIST

virile	oblivious	embellish	provocative	amorous
delude	pandemonium	seclusion	abhors	euphoria

1. When Elvis was recently discovered working in the produce section of a Memphis grocery, _____ broke out.

2. A well-known scientist reports receiving a text message from Big Foot that declares his greatest desire is _____ from curious tourists.

3. A(n) _____ couple was caught in an embarrassing position on a float in yesterday's Thanksgiving Day parade.

4. Townspeople could not believe it when Paul Owens, a _____ young man of twenty, lifted a house off of a child who was trapped underneath it.

5. Though her husband had been gone for six months, Mrs. Weller shockingly reports that she was _____ to his disappearance.

6. The _____ design of their new red leather uniforms is causing trouble for some police officers in a small California town.

7. The team's _____ on winning the state championships quickly disappeared when an alien spaceship landed and abducted their coach.

8. Dixie Lee Jean makes the startling prediction that a billionaire banker will _____ his wife about the real purpose of his business trips.

9. Which Latin teen idol recently announced that he _____ samba music?

10. Only film-star legend Maggie Gabor would dare to _____ the site of her eighth wedding with fifty varieties of flowers, one thousand pink balloons, and a dozen peacocks.

Word Visions

Identify the two vocabulary words represented in the drawings.

1. _____

2. _____

3 Write the vocabulary word on the line next to the situation it best illustrates. Use each word once. Imagine each scene begins with "When a person…"

Set One

> **VOCABULARY LIST**
>
> amorous　　　　abhor　　　　euphoria　　　　delude　　　　oblivious

1. wins the lottery _____
2. has to stand in a long line _____
3. crosses the street in front of a car _____
4. thinks he or she can write a great research paper in an hour _____
5. feels like cuddling with a sweetheart _____

Set Two

> **VOCABULARY LIST**
>
> embellish　　　　seclusion　　　　pandemonium　　　　virile　　　　provocative

6. wants to spend the summer in a cabin in the woods _____
7. starts bullfighting _____
8. says that the walk to the corner store was fifty miles, all uphill, through fields of cactus, in the burning sun _____
9. asks whether all drugs should be legal _____
10. is faced with a room full of five-year-olds at a birthday party _____

Word Wise

Collocations

At the *precise moment* I was thinking of calling Adela, the phone rang, and she was on the line. (Chapter 6)

I was *oblivious to* the conflicts that would result when I invited Karl to dinner. During dessert, he asked a *provocative question*, and everyone spent the rest of the evening arguing about whether nude sunbathing should be allowed on our beaches. (Chapter 7)

Word Pairs

Dissent/Assent: Dissent (Chapter 6) means "to differ in feeling or opinion." Assent (Chapter 8) means "to agree or concur." Sam had to dissent from the majority opinion because he felt the way to slow people down was a new stop sign, not lowering the speed limit. Samantha assented to the plan to lower the speed limit because she agreed with the rest of the council that that was the best way to slow traffic near the school.

Interactive Exercise

Put yourself in the author's chair by answering the following questions.

1. What kind of pandemonium breaks out when the door is opened?

    _____

2. If Byron had time to embellish his story, who would he say is chasing him?

    _____

3. What virile activities will they need to engage in to escape?

    _____

4. Has Byron deluded Estella about anything?

    _____

5. What kinds of danger will the couple have to be oblivious to in order to succeed?

    _____

6. What provocative question will Byron ask Estella at some point in their adventure?

    _____

7. Where do they go to find seclusion?

    _____

8. Will Byron and Estella have any amorous meetings during their escape?

    _____

9. Will they abhor or love each other when their adventure is over? Why?

    _____

10. Will they find euphoria or tragedy at the end of the story? Explain.

    _____

HINT

More Choices

If you want to read more for pleasure, here are some excellent writers of science fiction, romance, and mysteries to get you started:

Science Fiction

Isaac Asimov	*The Foundation Trilogy; I, Robot*
Ray Bradbury	*Fahrenheit 451; The Martian Chronicles*
Ursula K. Le Guin	*The Left Hand of Darkness; The Dispossessed*

Romance

Jane Austen	*Pride and Prejudice; Emma*
Laura Esquivel	*Like Water for Chocolate; Swift As Desire*
Thomas Hardy	*Return of the Native; Tess of the D'Urbervilles*

Mysteries

Agatha Christie	*Murder on the Orient Express; And Then There Were None*
Tony Hillerman	*A Thief of Time; The Dance Hall of the Dead*
Walter Mosley	*Devil in a Blue Dress; A Little Yellow Dog*

Word List

abhor
[ab hôrʹ]

v. to detest; to loathe; to hate

amorous
[amʹ ər əs]

adj. being in love; passionate

delude
[di lo͞odʹ]

v. to mislead; to deceive; to fool

embellish
[em belʹ ish, im-]

v. 1. to exaggerate; to elaborate; to add details
2. to decorate

euphoria
[yo͞o fôrʹ ē ə, -fōrʹ ē ə]

n. a feeling of extreme well-being or extreme happiness

oblivious
[ə blivʹ ē əs]

adj. unaware; forgetful

pandemonium
[panʹ də mōʹ nē əm]

n. disorder; chaos

provocative
[prə vokʹ ə tiv]

adj. stimulating; exciting; troubling

seclusion
[si klo͞oʹ zhən]

n. solitude; a sheltered or isolated place

virile
[vērʹ əl]

adj. masculine; manly; strong

Words to Watch

Which words would you like to practice with a bit more? Pick 3–5 words to study, and list them below. Write the word and its definition, and compose your own sentence using the word correctly. This extra practice could be the final touch to learning a word.

Word	Definition	Your Sentence
1.		
2.		
3.		
4.		
5.		

Chapter 8

Mystery

Missing from the Mound

I had **misgivings** about accepting this case from the beginning. I'm not much of a sports fan, so I wasn't sure I was the right detec-

5 tive to go looking for a missing pitcher. But an old friend of mine was working PR for the team, and she knew I would keep the case a secret. The team didn't want

10 anyone to find out its star pitcher was missing three days before the playoffs began. I promised Tess that I would keep my investigation **covert**. It was going to make

15 it more difficult to question people, but I'd manage.

My first call was to the pitcher's wife. She quickly **assented** to an interview in a bar near the stadium. I had a **presentiment** that the interview wasn't going to go smoothly. By the time I arrived, she looked to be drowning her sorrows in her fifth or sixth martini. I asked about her husband's activities the day he went missing. She started rambling about their marital problems and how he wasn't

20 any good to her. When she got to the point, I found out that they'd had a huge fight that morning about an affair he'd been having with the team owner's daughter. He stormed out of the house, and she hadn't seen him since.

I decided to **circumvent** the usual routes to meeting Lola McCurvy, the owner's daughter, by staking out her favorite beauty salon. I don't like to deal with a lot of personal assistants and such

25 when I need to talk to someone. Miss McCurvy seemed quite **incredulous** that I would want to speak with her about Thompson.

"Why talk to me? My relationship with George was a **transitory** affair. It only lasted for a couple of months. I dumped him over three weeks ago," she purred.

"What were you doing Monday between 10 a.m. and 8 p.m.?" I asked.

30 "If you are asking if I have an **alibi**, I'm afraid it isn't a great one. I wasn't feeling well that day, so I stayed home in bed. My maid came in a couple of times to bring me a cup of tea and a snack. You can check with her."

"Oh, I will."

I'm usually an **optimist**, which is rare for a PI, but I was beginning to doubt whether I'd find

35 Thompson before the playoffs began, and if I did, whether he'd be alive. I was going to have to take **decisive** steps to track him down. I needed to interview his teammates one by one, starting with the first baseman, Hernandez. It was widely known that he and Thompson had a strong aversion to each other. It was going to be a long day.

Predicting

For each set, write the definition on the line next to the word to which it belongs. If you are unsure, return to the reading, and underline any context clues you find. After you've made your predictions, check your answers against the Word List at the end of the chapter. Place a checkmark in the box next to each word whose definition you missed. These are the words you'll want to study closely.

Set One

agreed   feelings of doubt   to go around   secret   a feeling that something is about to happen

❑ 1. **misgivings** (line 1) _____

❑ 2. **covert** (line 14) _____

❑ 3. **assented** (line 16) _____

❑ 4. **presentiment** (line 17) _____

❑ 5. **circumvent** (line 23) _____

Set Two

a person who looks on the bright side   sure   temporary   disbelieving   an excuse or explanation

❑ 6. **incredulous** (line 25) _____

❑ 7. **transitory** (line 27) _____

❑ 8. **alibi** (line 30) _____

❑ 9. **optimist** (line 34) _____

❑ 10. **decisive** (line 36) _____

Self-Tests

MyReadingLab Visit Chapter 8: Mystery in MyReadingLab to complete the Self-Test activities.

1 Circle the correct word to complete each sentence.

1. The woman was certainly (decisive, incredulous). She decided on the color to paint her bathroom after looking at three samples for two minutes.

2. The operation was (transitory, covert), so Gerry couldn't tell any of his friends about his mission.

3. As the leaves fall off the trees, I am reminded of the (decisive, transitory) beauty of autumn.

4. It is good to be (incredulous, covert) when someone says you can easily get rich.

5. I had a great (presentiment, alibi): I was speaking in front of two hundred people when the robbery took place.

6. Most people would (assent, optimist) to being given a million dollars.

7. Anil tried to avoid taking a placement test; he wanted to (covert, circumvent) the college's procedures.

8. After Meiling found out her fiancé had cheated on her, she had (misgivings, assent) about marrying him.

9. Flor was nervous about getting in the car. She had a (presentiment, circumvent) that she would be in an accident.

10. Eddy is the eternal (alibi, optimist). Even when it is pouring rain, he is sure that it will clear up in time for a picnic.

2 Detectives often have questions or other thoughts running through their minds when they're trying to solve a crime. Write the vocabulary word that connects to the following thoughts the private investigator has about the case. Context clues are underlined to help you. Use each word once.

> **VOCABULARY LIST**
>
> | | | | | |
> |---|---|---|---|---|
> | alibi | presentiment | circumvent | covert | decisive |
> | assent | incredulous | misgiving | optimist | transitory |

1. I'm glad the witness <u>agreed</u> to be interviewed. _____
2. I'm <u>skeptical</u> that Thompson's wife told me the whole story about their fight. _____
3. The team manager <u>was in meetings Monday from 8 a.m. until 10 p.m.</u> _____
4. I need to find a way <u>to avoid</u> the security guard so I can look around the locker room undisturbed. _____
5. I <u>really feel like I will find Thompson tomorrow.</u> _____
6. Did Thompson disappear because he had <u>a feeling that something bad was about to happen</u>? _____
7. I may have to <u>conceal</u> myself somewhere in the clubhouse to discover any team secrets. _____
8. Interviewing the team owner alone is <u>crucial</u> to solving this mystery. I think he knows more than he wanted to share when the coach was around. _____
9. I need to search Thompson's locker right away because things <u>may change quickly</u> if anyone discovers he is missing. _____
10. Why do I <u>distrust</u> Miss McCurvy's story that the maid brought her tea? _____

3 Finish the story using the vocabulary words. Use each word once.

> **VOCABULARY LIST**
>
> | | | | | |
> |---|---|---|---|---|
> | alibi | transitory | assented | misgivings | optimist |
> | circumvent | covert | decisive | incredulous | presentiment |

I had a(n) (1)_____ that something bad was going to happen while we were on vacation. My wife thought my (2)_____ were silly, but after I kept on about them for three days, she (3)_____ to going home early. When we got home, we were shocked that all our living room furniture was missing. At first my wife was (4)_____. She was sure it was a joke by a neighbor, but I finally convinced her that we had been robbed. The police were great. They took (5)_____ action and started interviewing the neighbors right away. It must have been a(n) (6)_____ operation. No one saw anyone near our house. Even the sneaky kid down the street had a(n) (7)_____. He was visiting his grandmother two states away all the time we were gone. It was no time to try to (8)_____ usual

procedures, so I called the insurance company to get the paperwork started. I guess I should take my wife's view that possessions are only (9)_____. In fact, she is such a(n) (10)_____ that she now sees the robbery as a great chance to redecorate the house.

Identify the two vocabulary words represented in the photos.

1. _____

2. _____

Word Wise

Collocations

The river was rising; it was time for *decisive action* or most of the town would be flooded. The citizens quickly banded together to fill the sandbags. (Chapter 8)

Andres is the *eternal optimist*. Though Veronica has turned him down twenty times, he still believes she will change her mind and one day go out with him. (Chapter 8)

Word Pairs

Covert/Overt: Covert (Chapter 8) means "concealed; secret," while overt means "open; not concealed." Tim's covert feelings for Leslie were in danger of being revealed when he dropped a love note he had written her but never planned to deliver. Tom was so overt with his feelings that Leslie was embarrassed when he announced his love for her over the loud speaker at school.

Connotations and Denotations

Optimist (Chapter 8): denotation—"a person who looks on the bright side." When some people think of an optimist, they picture a cheery, positive person. For other people, the word *optimist* connotes a person who refuses to face the harsher aspects of life. Which way do you see the optimist?

Interesting Etymologies

Alibi (Chapter 8) comes from Latin *alibi*, meaning "elsewhere." It is a reason a person uses to say he or she couldn't have committed a crime because the person was somewhere besides where the crime was committed. It has its roots in the Latin *alius*, or "(an)other," such as in the word alias, meaning "another, or false, name."

Interactive Exercise

List two situations that could be relevant to each word.

EXAMPLE: presentiment—not wanting to answer the phone (due to a feeling that the call will bring sad news); deciding not to board an airplane (because of a feeling that something bad will happen)

1. presentiment

   _____   _____

2. circumvent

   _____   _____

3. incredulous

   _____   _____

4. covert

   _____   _____

5. misgiving

   _____   _____

6. alibi

   _____   _____

7. transitory

   _____   _____

8. optimist

   _____   _____

9. assent

   _____   _____

10. decisive

   _____   _____

Conversation Starters

An excellent way to review the vocabulary words and help to make them your own is to use them when you are speaking. Gather three to five friends or classmates, and use one or more of the conversation starters below. Before you begin talking, have each person write down six of the vocabulary words he or she will use during the conversation. Share your lists with each other to check that you did not all pick the same six words. Try to cover all of the words you want to study, whether you are reviewing one, two, or more chapters.

1. Imagine living on a spaceship for months, or even years. What would be some positives and negatives to such a life? Would you want to do that?
2. How does Estella and Byron's relationship compare to others you have seen (real or fictitious)?
3. What are some possible things that could have happened to Thompson?
4. What book or movie would you recommend to a friend? What type of book or movie is it, such as a romance or mystery? What elements make it worth reading or seeing?

Word List

alibi
[al′ ə bī′]

n. an excuse or explanation, especially used to avoid blame

assent
[ə sent′]

v. to agree or concur

n. agreement, as to a proposal

circumvent
[sûr′ kəm vent′;
sûr′ kəm vent′]

v. 1. to go around
2. to avoid by cleverness; to elude

covert
[kō′ vərt]

adj. concealed; secret; disguised

decisive
[di sī′ siv]

adj. 1. displaying firmness; determined; sure
2. crucial; important

incredulous
[in krej′ ə ləs]

adj. skeptical; doubtful; disbelieving

misgiving
[mis giv′ ing]

n. a feeling of doubt or distrust

optimist
[op′ tə mist]

n. a person who looks on the bright side; one who expects a positive result

presentiment
[pri zen′ tə mənt]

n. a feeling that something is about to happen, especially something bad; foreboding; expectation

transitory
[tran′ si tôr′ ē]

adj. not lasting; temporary

Words to Watch

Which words would you like to practice with a bit more? Pick 3–5 words to study, and list them below. Write the word and its definition, and compose your own sentence using the word correctly. This extra practice could be the final touch to learning a word.

Word	Definition	Your Sentence
1. _____	_____	_____
		_____
2. _____	_____	_____
		_____
3. _____	_____	_____
		_____
4. _____	_____	_____
		_____
5. _____	_____	_____
		_____

Chapter 9

Word Parts II

Look for words with these **prefixes**, **roots**, and/or **suffixes** as you work through this book. You may have already seen some of them, and you will see others in later chapters. Learning basic word parts can help you figure out the meanings of unfamiliar words.

prefix: a word part added to the beginning of a word that changes the meaning of the root

root: a word's basic part with its essential meaning

suffix: a word part added to the end of a word; indicates the part of speech

Word Part	Meaning	Examples and Definitions
Prefixes		
mis-	wrong	*misconstrue:* to get the wrong idea *misgiving:* a feeling that something is wrong
sub-, sup-	below, under	*submerge:* to put below water *suppress:* to keep under control
trans-	across	*transfer:* to carry across *transatlantic:* going across the Atlantic
Roots		
-cred-	believe, trust	*credibility:* believability *credentials:* evidence of one's right to be trusted
-opt-	best	*optimist:* a person who sees the best in things *optimism:* the practice of looking for the best in situations
-pend-, -pens-	hang, weigh, pay	*suspend:* to hang *pensive:* weighing an idea; thoughtful
-sens-, -sent-	feel, be aware	*consensus:* an opinion where people feel the same way *dissent:* to differ in feeling
-vers-, -vert-	turn	*versatile:* capable of turning easily from one task to another *avert:* to turn away
Suffixes		
-ism (makes a noun)	action, practice, theory	*colloquialism:* the action of using informal language *patriotism:* the practice of loving one's country
-ist (makes a noun)	a person who	*naturalist:* a person who is an expert on plant or animal life *columnist:* a person who writes a column

1 Read each definition, and choose the appropriate word from the list below. Use each word once. The meaning of the word part is underlined to help you make the connection. Refer to the Word Parts list if you need help.

VOCABULARY LIST

optimize	misuse	zoologist	expensive	subterranean
controversy	transmit	credible	sensitive	plagiarism

1. to operate the <u>wrong</u> way _____
2. <u>turn</u> against; an argument _____
3. capable of being <u>believed</u> _____
4. the <u>action</u> of using another's words as one's own _____
5. to make the <u>best</u> use of _____
6. to send <u>across</u> _____
7. <u>paying</u> a lot for _____
8. <u>underground</u> _____
9. <u>a person who</u> studies animals _____
10. <u>be aware</u> of other people's views and feelings _____

2 Finish the sentences with the meaning of each word part. Use each meaning once. The word part is underlined to help you make the connection.

VOCABULARY LIST

below	feels	across	wrong	turn
practice	best	trusts	hanging	a person who

1. A <u>senti</u>mental person _____ strongly about old items.
2. If you make a <u>mis</u>take, you do the _____ thing.
3. When a company gives a person <u>cred</u>it, it _____ that the person will pay his or her bills.
4. A <u>sub</u>ordinate works _____ his or her boss.
5. Rac<u>ism</u> is the _____ of believing one's ethnic background is better than other people's.
6. The child wanted to di<u>vert</u> attention from the mess he had made, so he tried to _____ his mother's interest to the sound of a siren out front.
7. The diamond <u>pend</u>ant was _____ around her neck.
8. People often need to <u>trans</u>fer from one bus to another when they take a trip _____ town.
9. A solo<u>ist</u> is _____ performs alone.
10. June's <u>optim</u>ism makes her fun to be around; she always looks for the _____ in a situation, even when it is easy to see the worst.

3 Finish the story using the word parts below. Use each word part once. Your knowledge of word parts, as well as the context clues, will help you create the correct words. If you do not understand the meaning of a word you have made, check your dictionary for the definition or to see whether the word exists.

WORD PARTS

trans	pend	ist	vert	cred
sup	ism	mis	opt	sent

All Fired Up

My excursion to the art gallery became quite an adventure. While I was looking at a sculpture, a fire alarm sounded. I hurried outside. Lingering out front, I heard a rumor that an arson(1)_____ had started the fire. I have been studying criminology, so I began talking with people to discover any motives. They didn't (2)_____press their opinions. I heard that one of the gallery owners, Pierre, and his wife were having problems. I also discovered that Pierre's business partner had several gambling debts. Problems in Pierre's life seemed to be omnipresent.

Then I heard a man shout, *"C'est une catastrophe!"* It was Pierre; he was in shock. It seemed like the (3)_____imal time to offer my assistance. I told him he could de(4)_____ on me for help because I was going to be an insurance investigator, and I had studied similar cases in college. Pierre con(5)_____ed to my helping him. While we waited to return to the gallery, we talked about the (6)_____itory nature of life, which seemed to calm Pierre a bit.

After the fire was out, we went in to survey the damage. It was in(7)_____ible, but only one painting was seriously damaged. When Pierre began to pick up bits of the frame, I told him to be careful not to disturb any evidence. If we (8)_____handled the situation at the beginning, we would never find what caused the fire. Pierre began to complain that we would never discover who tried to ruin him. Just when his pessim(9)_____ was at its greatest, I noticed wax on a nearby table. Pierre's eyes lit up—he had inad(10)_____ently set a candle there when he had gone to answer the phone. We had found the guilty party.

4 Pick the best definition for each underlined word using your knowledge of word parts. Circle the word part in each of the underlined words.

a. best or most favorable

f. a person who commits blackmail

b. to feel angry

g. evidence that one is qualified or can be trusted

c. to weigh, prepare, and give out

h. a turning away; hatred

d. below the required level

i. the action of putting great value on objects

e. crossing the sea

j. given wrong information

_____ 1. Because Larry's work for the last three months had been <u>substandard</u>, his boss called him in to see what was wrong.

_____ 2. The reporter showed his <u>credentials</u> to gain access to the crime scene.

_____ 3. For <u>optimum</u> results, I study early in the morning when I can clearly focus my mind.

_____ 4. The <u>transoceanic</u> voyage took us a week. It was a peaceful vacation.

_____ 5. We were <u>misinformed</u> about the meeting. We thought it began at three o'clock, but it really began at two.

_____ 6. Because a new shipment of the drug had just arrived, the pharmacy was able to <u>dispense</u> my medicine within two hours of the prescription being written.

_____ 7. I have an <u>aversion</u> to getting up early. I could easily sleep until ten o'clock every morning.

_____ 8. I <u>resent</u> that I did all the work while my colleagues got all the credit.

_____ 9. The family's <u>materialism</u> led to financial problems; they couldn't afford everything they bought.

_____ 10. The <u>extortionist</u> asked for $10,000 to be delivered by noon the next day or he would reveal the mayor's secret.

5 A good way to remember word parts is to pick one word that uses a word part and understand how that word part functions in the word. Then you can apply that meaning to other words that have the same word part. Use the following words to help you match the word part to its meaning.

Set One

_____ 1. **mis-:** misgivings, mislead, mistake

a. best

_____ 2. **sub-, sup-:** submerge, submissive, suppress

b. feel, be aware

_____ 3. **-cred-:** credibility, incredible, credit

c. below, under

_____ 4. **-opt-:** optimist, optimum, optimize

d. wrong

_____ 5. **-sens-, -sent-:** consensus, sentimental, dissent

e. believe, trust

Set Two

_____ 6. **trans-:** transfer, translate, transitory

f. a person who

_____ 7. **-vers-, -vert-:** aversion, covert, avert

g. across

_____ 8. **-ist:** naturalist, optimist, artist

h. action, practice, theory

_____ 9. **-pend-, -pens-:** suspend, dependable, expensive

i. turn

_____ 10. **-ism:** patriotism, optimism, colloquialism

j. hang, weigh, pay

Interactive Exercise

Use the dictionary to find a word you don't know that uses each word part listed below. Write the meaning of the word part, the word, and the definition. If your dictionary has the etymology (history) of the word, see how the word part relates to the meaning, and write the etymology after the definition.

Word Part	Meaning	Word	Definition and Etymology
EXAMPLE:			
-pend-	hang	pendulous	1. hanging loosely
			2. undecided
			Latin "pendulus," from "pendere," hang
1. *mis-*			
2. *sub-*			
3. *trans-*			
4. *-cred-*			
5. *-sent-*			

HINT

Tips for Enjoying a Novel or Short Story

Readers enjoy a book more when they become involved with it. Try to put yourself in the novel or short story by imagining yourself in a character's situation. What would you do if you had to stop an alien invasion, cope with a broken heart, or solve a murder? Learn to appreciate the descriptions of the places in the story. Try to visualize yourself hiking through the jungle, cooking a big meal in the kitchen, or hiding under a bed. Look for the author's message as you read. Ask yourself what point the author is trying to get across. Do you agree or disagree with the author's point? By putting yourself in the story and thinking about the significance of events, you will want to keep reading to see what happens to the characters because now they and their world are a part of you.

Match each photograph to one of the word parts below, and write the meaning of the word part.

mis-   sub-/sup-   -cred-   -pend-/-pens-   -ist

1. _____

2. _____

Word Wise

Internet Activity: How Often Is It Used?

Here is an activity that will illustrate different contexts for the vocabulary words and emphasize the enormity of the Internet. Type a vocabulary word into a search engine such as Google, Bing, or Yahoo. Note how many times the word is found. Read through the first few entries and see how the word is used. Find a Web site that seems interesting. Open it and look for the word again to view it in its full context. For example, the word *amiable* turned up 22,100,000 results. Among the first few entries, it was used in the contexts of defining the word, providing quotations that use the word, listing songs for those in an amiable mood, and describing personality types. Sometimes you will get a lot more results. *Covert* turned up 52,300,000 results. And sometimes the results can be surprising. For *lax,* several of the 72,700,000 results had to deal with LAX (Los Angeles International Airport) and quite a few with lacrosse. Have fun seeing what is out there.

Your word: _____

Number of results: _____

A sample context: _____

Name or address (URL) of the Web site you visited: _____

Share your finds with classmates. What words did people pick to look up? Which had the least results, and which had the most? Did anyone find a really interesting site?

Chapter 10

Review

Focus on Chapters 6–9

The following activities give you the opportunity to further interact with the vocabulary words you've been learning. By taking tests, answering questions, using visuals, doing a crossword puzzle, and working with others, you will see which words you know well and which ones need additional study.

Self-Tests MyReadingLab Visit Chapter 10: Review in MyReadingLab to complete the Self-Test activities.

LO 4,8 **1** Match each term with its synonym in Set One and its antonym in Set Two.

Synonyms

Set One

_____ 1. pandemonium a. elaborate

_____ 2. embellish b. chaos

_____ 3. delude c. dislike

_____ 4. antipathy d. explanation

_____ 5. alibi e. mislead

Antonyms

Set Two

_____ 6. condone f. protect

_____ 7. annihilate g. disagree

_____ 8. provocative h. face

_____ 9. circumvent i. punish

_____ 10. assent j. comforting

Remember to add words to Word Reactions on page 175 after completing the Review chapter activities.

LO 1 **2** Pick the word that best completes each sentence.

1. The battle was a(n) _____ one; the next day the enemy surrendered.

   a. incredulous   b. oblivious   c. decisive   d. cursory

2. It is easy to see how much Nina _____ housework because dust covers all her furniture.

   a. abhors   b. condones   c. assents   d. subjugates

3. The king considered himself _____ until the ruler in the next kingdom sent ten thousand knights into battle against him.

   a. cursory   b. amorous   c. covert   d. omnipotent

4. The man stayed _____ through daily exercise and a healthy diet.

   a. precise   b. provocative   c. transitory   d. virile

5. An accountant needs to be _____. There can be big problems if the numbers don't add up correctly.

   a. omnipotent   b. covert   c. precise   d. virile

6. The romantic music put the couple in a(n) _____ mood.

   a. oblivious   b. amorous   c. decisive   d. omnipotent

7. The _____ reported back to the president that trouble was looming in several countries in Africa.

   a. optimist   b. omnipotent   c. emissary   d. pandemonium

8. I had a(n) _____ that class was going to be cancelled, and I was right. A fire in the chemistry lab closed several buildings.

   a. euphoria   b. presentiment   c. antipathy   d. alibi

LO 1 **3** Pick the vocabulary word that best completes the sentence. Use each word once.

pandemonium	alibi	seclusion	optimist	dissent

1. Dave didn't have a good _____. The restaurant he said he had been at the night of the robbery was closed for repairs at the time.

2. After having guests for four weeks, I was looking forward to a bit of _____ while camping out in the desert.

3. There was a lot of _____ at the meeting over raising the dues $100 to cover the cost of adding a new parking area.

4. I was shocked at the _____ in the classroom when I returned. I had only run across the hall to borrow a marker from another teacher, and the classroom was in chaos when I returned.

5. I try to be a(n) _____, but when everything is going wrong, it is hard to see the best in things.

4 Complete the following sentences that illustrate collocations. The rest of the collocation is in italics. Use each word once.

precise	oblivious	decisive	cursory	provocative	optimist

1. After a _____ *inspection* of the report, my boss said it was fine, and he ran out the door.

2. Lin is an *eternal* _____. Even when a plant is nothing but a shriveled twig, she believes it could come back to life.

3. Lucinda and Minh were talking on the corner, _____ *to* the fight brewing a few feet away from them.

4. At the _____ *moment* I should have been starting my speech, I was instead talking to a police officer on why I was speeding.

5. After the shoplifter ran out of the store, our manager took _____ *action* and followed him out to the parking lot to get the license plate number of the man's car.

6. I was surprised by Mac's _____ *question* on whether I would ever eat worms or crickets. I wondered what was in the dish he had just served me.

5 Fill in the missing word part, and circle the meaning of the word part found in each sentence.

sub	trans	sent	eu	cred	mis	vert	opt

1. I didn't believe a word Carlos said. I couldn't be anything but in_____ulous when someone tells me that my neighbors are a vampire and a werewolf.

2. The conqueror tried to _____jugate all of the people, but there were too many to easily put them under one person's rule.

3. I had several _____givings about having a picnic in February, but surprisingly nothing went wrong and everyone had a good time outside.

4. When you come across people for just a few days or weeks, you realize that there are relationships that are meant to be _____itory.

5. My _____phoria at winning the writing contest was long lasting. I felt so good I couldn't stop smiling, laughing, and hugging people for a month.

6. I told my friends that I would have to dis_____; I didn't feel our history instructor was giving us too much homework.

7. I try to be a(n) _____imist when I meet new people. I like to think the best about people until they do something to show me otherwise.

8. My mission to find out what my cousin was doing at the mall every day was supposed to be a co_____ one, so I had to turn away and hide behind a rack of shirts when she suddenly headed in my direction.

VOCABULARY LIST

amorous	assent	misgivings	covert	cursory
delude	oblivious	miscalculated	condone	transitory

A Winter Plan

I had some (1)_____ when my girlfriend called and wanted me to come over just as the snowstorm was beginning. She said she was feeling lonely and (2)_____. I hated to disappoint her. I took a(n) (3)_____ look outside. From my peak out the window, I didn't think it looked too bad yet. It is easy to (4)_____ oneself when love is involved. All of a sudden I became (5)_____ to the possible dangers of traveling on icy roads or trying to get through streets covered with snow. I knew none of my friends would (6)_____ such reckless behavior, so I didn't call anyone to say where I was going. This was going to be my (7)_____ operation of love.

Just as I was tying my boots, the phone rang again. It was my girlfriend calling to say that she had (8)_____ the strength of the storm, and she didn't think I should come. I protested at first, but I finally had to (9)_____ when I saw that she was right about endangering my life. She told me that her love for me wasn't (10)_____ but that bad weather was. We would be together again in just a couple of days.

Interactive Exercise

LO 2 Answer the following questions to further test your understanding of the vocabulary words.

1. What procedure would you like to circumvent? Why?

   _____

   _____

2. What are two methods people have used to subjugate other people?

   _____

   _____

3. What are two things you have an antipathy toward?

   _____

   _____

4. How might someone embellish a story about a game or contest he or she was in?

   _____

   _____

5. Give an example of a statement you would be incredulous about.

   _____

6. What is something you have had a presentiment about?

   _____

7. Where would you like to be sent as an emissary? Why would you like to go there?

   _____

   _____

8. What are two kinds of experiences that can cause euphoria?

   _____

   _____

9. What is something you would like to annihilate? Why?

   _____

   _____

10. Where do you go (or could you go) when you are looking for seclusion?

    _____

    _____

LO 6 **Art Gallery**

Within the rectangles draw a picture for six of the words
below. Your artwork can be simple and even use stick figures.

Your goal is to remember the words by envisioning your own interpretation of them. Your instructor may ask you to redo one of your drawings on a larger sheet of paper. The larger drawings can be shared with the whole class to see if people can guess what words they represent. Suggestion: Before you write the words on the lines below, switch pages with a classmate to see if he or she can identify the word each drawing shows.

Alternate method: Use your own photos, magazines, or the Internet to find photographs that illustrate six of the words. Print, photocopy, or cut out the photos (if you own the magazines), and bring them to class. Or you can mix and match the two methods.

VOCABULARY LIST

condone	emissary	miscalculation	omnipotent	subjugate
abhor	embellish	oblivious	seclusion	virile
assent	circumvent	covert	optimist	transitory

1. _____

2. _____

3. _____

4. _____

5. _____

6. _____

Crossword Puzzle LO 3

Across

2. "I detest that style."
4. an outfit or a question, as examples
7. a feeling of doubt or distrust
8. feeling one should have on one's wedding day
9. "I don't believe your story."
12. the way a spy should do things
13. to fool
15. hasty
16. during an earthquake, for example
17. having unlimited authority
19. foreboding

Down

1. the opposite of fondness
2. to destroy
3. "I don't feel the same way."
5. a weight lifter, for example
6. "Oops!"
10. displaying firmness or important
11. "I was with three friends all night."
14. passionate
18. accurate or demanding

Use the following words to complete the crossword puzzle. Use each word once.

VOCABULARY LIST

abhor	euphoria
alibi	incredulous
amorous	miscalculation
annihilate	misgiving
antipathy	omnipotent
covert	pandemonium
cursory	precise
decisive	presentiment
delude	provocative
dissent	virile

HINT

Read for Fun

It might sound obvious, but many people forget that reading for fun makes a person a better reader overall. If you think you don't like to read, search for reading material about a subject that interests you.

Assess your reading interests:

- Do you like to keep up on current events? Become a newspaper or newsmagazine reader.
- Do you have a hobby? Subscribe to a magazine on the topic.
- Do you like to look into people's lives? Pick up a collection of short stories or a novel. You can find everything from romance to mystery in fiction writing.
- Is there a time period you are interested in? Nonfiction and fiction books deal with events from the days of the dinosaurs to the unknown future.
- Are you interested in travel or different countries? Try books by authors from foreign lands.
- Do you like to read in short spurts or for long periods? Newspaper articles, essays, poetry, and short stories may appeal more to those who like to read a little at a time. Novels, plays, and nonfiction books may appeal more to those who like intricate tales.

Visit the library to try out different types of reading material. It's free! Also explore the Internet for various reading sources.

Finding the type of reading material that is right for your personality and interests will make reading fun, will lead to better reading skills, and will even make the reading you are required to do more productive.

Mix It Up LO 2,3,7

Making a Scene

Get together with six to nine classmates and divide into two to three groups. Each group creates a situation or uses one of the suggestions below to write a short scene using at least six of the vocabulary words to be studied. If you want to study several words, make sure each group doesn't pick the same six words. Each group acts out the scene, with the rest noting how the words are used. You may choose to emphasize the vocabulary words by your actions or tone of voice while doing the scene to help everyone remember the words. Discuss how the words fit in after the scene is completed. The scenes can also be done as role-playing with pairs creating the scenes instead of small groups. Creating scenes is an especially fun and useful activity if you like to act or enjoy movement.

The following are possible scenes related to specific chapters: crewmates discussing their new mission from Chapter 6, Estella's neighbors talking about all the noise at her place the night before from Chapter 7, and the baseball team in the locker room wondering where Thompson is just before the game is about to begin from Chapter 8. You can also use the overall section theme of Reading for Pleasure to create your own ideas using words from all three chapters.

If you enjoy this collaborative activity, remember to use it again when you are reviewing later chapters in this book. Have fun making the scenes, and you will enjoy the review process.

Part II

Academic Words

Page 88

Page 105

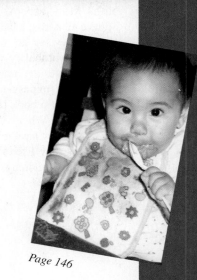

Page 146

Chapter 11

Education

Creating Readers

Reading is one of the essential skills in this world, and one that needs to be **nurtured** from an early age. The easiest way to **facilitate** reading development in children is to read to them aloud. When parents, grandparents, aunts, uncles, neighbors, or even older siblings take the time to read to children, children become interested in the reading process. Reading aloud to children can begin at a very young age, even within weeks of birth. Most experts recommend that parents **adhere** to at least a half hour a day of reading to a child to develop an interest in reading. Children hear new vocabulary when they are read to, and that stimulates the brain. A child's language skills can even **surpass** adult expectations when discussion of a book becomes part of the reading environment. When adults talk to children about the stories they have read—what happened, which characters they liked best, what the point of the story was—children's critical-thinking skills are greatly increased.

Adults shouldn't **impose** their reading interests or level on a child. Asking children to read books too far above their comprehension level can **impede** their reading development. The mastery of reading is tied to self-esteem, so parents want to make sure not to push their children. A simple way to see if a child wants to read a book is to take the child to the library or bookstore and let the child find books that interest him or her. An adult can guide a child's choices, especially based on the child's interests (animals, knights, the ocean), but the child should be excited about the books the family takes home to read. Children have an **innate** interest in language, and adults can support that natural interest through wise reading choices.

Parents can also be reading **advocates** by having books in the home and reading themselves. When a child sees a parent enjoy reading, the child learns that it is a fun and important skill to acquire. Today's children are so **susceptible** to the lure of television and video games (most children spend three to four hours a day in front of the television) that it is essential for parents to take the lead in making reading an exciting and memorable experience. All children have the **potential** to be successful readers. For some children, reading skills will come quickly and easily; for others, it will take more time. If parents are ever unsure about a child's reading ability, they can always contact school or community programs for advice.

Predicting

For each set, write the definition on the line next to the word to which it belongs. If you are unsure, return to the reading, and underline any context clues you find. After you've made your predictions, check your answers against the Word List at the end of the chapter. Place a checkmark in the box next to each word whose definition you missed. These are the words you'll want to study closely.

Set One

| to force on others | to make easier | encouraged | to go beyond | to follow closely |

❑ 1. **nurtured** (line 2) _____

❑ 2. **facilitate** (line 3) _____

❑ 3. **adhere** (line 11) _____

❑ 4. **surpass** (line 15) _____

❑ 5. **impose** (line 22) _____

Set Two

| open to an influence | to block | people who support a cause | the ability for growth | possessed at birth |

❑ 6. **impede** (line 25) _____

❑ 7. **innate** (line 36) _____

❑ 8. **advocates** (line 39) _____

❑ 9. **susceptible** (line 44) _____

❑ 10. **potential** (line 49) _____

Self-Tests

MyReadingLab   Visit Chapter 11: Education in MyReadingLab to complete the Self-Test activities.

1 In each group, there are three synonyms and one antonym. Circle the antonym.

1. impede	block	facilitate	obstruct
2. urge	oppose	advocate	recommend
3. force	impose	require	choose
4. grow	educate	hinder	nurture
5. assist	impede	help	facilitate
6. separate	adhere	stick	hold
7. exceed	surpass	fail	excel
8. natural	learned	inborn	innate
9. possible	unlikely	budding	potential
10. resistant	open	sensitive	susceptible

2 Finish the readings using the vocabulary words. Use each word once.

VOCABULARY LIST

impose	adhere	innate	impedes	potential
facilitates	surpassed	susceptible	advocate	nurtured

Set One

I (1)_____ to a steady reading plan. I get three books from the library every other week. My parents (2)_____ my love of reading when I was young. Every summer they would sign me up for the library's reading program. If I read ten books, I got a prize. Sometimes work (3)_____ my reading plan. I get busy with a project or come home so tired that I don't feel like reading. But those times are rare. I love to read, and having the library so close really (4)_____ my reading habit. There are so many great books there to choose from. I am such a(n) (5)_____ for the library that I have started volunteering to read during story time once a week. This week the kids get to hear *Penguin on the Lookout.* It is one of my favorites.

Set Two

I loved school, though I was (6)_____ to colds and missed more days than I wanted. I discovered I had a(n) (7)_____ talent for drawing in the second grade. I continued to do sketches of friends throughout school, and I enjoyed using watercolors in college. I minored in art, but I didn't think I really had the (8)_____ to become a famous artist. I didn't want to (9)_____ on my friends and family while I struggled to make it in the art world. Instead I (10)_____ my parents' expectations and went into medicine. In the field of medical research, I still get to draw sometimes, and maybe someday I can find a cure for the common cold so kids won't have to miss school like I did.

3 Complete the sentences using the vocabulary words. Use each word once.

VOCABULARY LIST

impeded	innate	susceptible	surpassed	facilitate
nurture	adhere	advocate	imposed	potential

1. I _____ to the idea of saving money for a happier future.

2. My _____ talents are in music and dance; I have always done well in those areas.

3. Community members strongly support _____ uses for the site as a library or park.

4. To _____ the moving process, I clearly labeled all the boxes.

5. The _____ appeared on the talk show to explain his views on why we need more land for parks.

6. Educators devote themselves to the safety and _____ of children in classrooms throughout the world.

7. The reading selections in my literature class have _____ my expectations: they are all fascinating.

8. My parents _____ a ten o'clock curfew on me when I was in high school.

9. Because I am _____ to illness, I like to wear a sweater when it is chilly.

10. Our plans were _____ by the rainy weather. We had to wait until the sun came out to play tennis.

Word Wise

Context Clue Mini-Lesson 3

This lesson uses examples to explain the unknown word. The example may consist of one illustration of the word or be a list of items. In the paragraph below, circle the examples you find that clarify the meaning of the underlined words. Then use the examples to write your own definitions on the lines next to the words that follow the paragraph.

The hotel was <u>palatial</u> with its spacious rooms, private hot tubs, balconies with ocean views, four swimming pools, three restaurants, and a disco. I couldn't believe I had won a free weekend. I enjoyed my afternoon <u>repast</u> of lobster, fresh fruit, a variety of salads, and chocolate cake. Now it was time for a relaxing nap. However, the <u>incessant</u> noise from outside began to bother me. Within twenty minutes of closing my eyes, music blared from the disco, a dog started barking, and a large group of people settled outside my window to chat. I was not going to let these annoyances <u>infringe</u> on my vacation, like I let Uncle Stephan do last year when we went fishing and he complained the whole time about the cold water. I decided my wisest move was to take a walk in the lovely garden and relax that way.

Your Definition

1. Palatial _____

2. Repast _____

3. Incessant _____

4. Infringe _____

Interactive Version: For each photograph write a blurb for the back cover of the book on which the photograph would appear on the front cover. You can create a title or author for each book and decide whether the book is fiction or nonfiction. Use at least three of the vocabulary words in each blurb.

EXAMPLE:
Gardening Basics nurtures the innate gardener in all of us. The book advocates simple gardening practices that are easy to adhere to. With this book you will surpass your expectations on how beautiful your yard can be!

Blurb 1:

_____

_____

_____

_____

_____

_____

Blurb 2:

_____

_____

_____

_____

_____

_____

Word Part Reminder

Below are a few exercises to help you review the word parts you have been learning. Fill in the missing word part from the list, and circle the meaning of the word part found in each sentence. Try to complete the questions without returning to the Word Parts chapter, but if you get stuck, look back at Chapter 9.

sent	mis	ist	pens

1. My cousin is a person who loves music, so I suggested he become a pian_____.

2. I signed the con_____ form because I feel it is important for my kids to learn how to swim.

3. Suzy doesn't usually do anything wrong when I babysit her, but today she was in a mood to _____behave.

4. It was more than I wanted to pay; I thought $50 was too ex_____ive for a ripped poster even if it was of my favorite band.

Word List

adhere
[ad hēr′]

v. 1. to follow closely, such as a plan; to support something
2. to stick together; to hold

advocate
n. [ad′ və kit]

v. [ad′ və kāt′]

n. a person who supports a cause

v. to support or urge; to recommend

facilitate
[fə sil′ ə tāt′]

v. to make easier; to assist

impede
[im pēd′]

v. to block; to hinder

impose
[im pōz′]

v. to force on others

innate
[i nāt′, in′ āt′]

adj. 1. possessed at birth; natural
2. possessed as an essential trait

nurture
[nûr′ chər]

v. to encourage; to educate or train

n. the act of promoting growth; rearing

potential
[pə ten′ shəl]

n. the ability for growth or development

adj. possible but not yet realized

surpass
[sər pas′]

v. to go beyond; to excel; to be superior to

susceptible
[sə sep′ tə bəl]

adj. open to an influence; sensitive

Words to Watch

Which words would you like to practice with a bit more? Pick 3–5 words to study, and list them below. Write the word and its definition, and compose your own sentence using the word correctly. This extra practice could be the final touch to learning a word.

Word	Definition	Your Sentence
1.		
2.		
3.		
4.		
5.		

Chapter 12

Environmental Science

Endangered Animals

The International Union for the Conservation of Nature and Natural Resources (IUCN) has a list of endangered plants and animals known as the Red List. Animals on the list range from the well-known lowland gorilla to the lesser-known
5 aye-aye. Within the "threatened" category, animals are listed as "critically endangered," "endangered," or "vulnerable." **Conservationists** hope the list will heighten public awareness of the dangers animals face and **elicit** responses on ways to save these animals.

10 The giant panda, a symbol for endangered animals, is **endemic** to Southwest China. The panda eats about twenty to forty pounds of bamboo a day. As human populations grow, animals lose more of their natural **habitat**. Forests and grasslands are being destroyed for timber, agriculture, and housing expansion. The giant panda's habitat is diminishing due to **encroachment** for agriculture and timber needs. The Chinese government has established more
15 than fifty panda reserves, which shields almost 60 percent of the current population. Estimates place about 1,800 pandas in the wild.

The babirusa, or wild pig, found on Sulawesi and other Indonesian islands is listed as vulnerable. The unusual-looking babirusa has two sets of tusks, one of which grows on the top of the snout and curves back toward the animal's forehead. The babirusa is **omnivorous**, eating fruit, leaves, and
20 small animals. Though protected, hunting contributes to the animal's decline. They are killed for food, and their unusual skulls are found in local markets for sale to tourists. In the last census, only 5,000 babirusa were found in the wild.

The blue whale, found in every ocean, is listed as endangered. The largest **mammal** on Earth, blue whales are usually
25 80 to 100 feet long and weigh more than 100 tons. They eat about 8,000 pounds a day of krill, a shrimp-like animal. Before the whaling era, population estimates were close to 250,000 animals. About 99 percent were killed due to whaling. In 1966, the International Whaling Commission put a **moratorium** on
30 hunting blue whales. Current estimates place the blue whale population between 10,000 and 25,000. Blue whales now face threats from pollution, including increases in ocean noise levels (possibly interfering with their low-frequency communication) and global warming (disrupting migration patterns and
35 altering food supplies).

These examples illustrate the major threats animals face: habitat loss, hunting, and pollution. The field of **zoology** has helped people learn more about animals. With this knowledge and by working together, individuals and governments can
40 **avert** the loss of today's threatened animals.

Predicting

For each set, write the definition on the line next to the word to which it belongs. If you are unsure, return to the reading, and underline any context clues you find. After you've made your predictions, check your answers against the Word List at the end of the chapter. Place a checkmark in the box next to each word whose definition you missed. These are the words you'll want to study closely.

Set One

to draw or bring out   an intrusion   the environment where a plant or animal typically lives

natural to a particular area   people who work to save the environment

❑ 1. **conservationists** (line 7) _____

❑ 2. **elicit** (line 8) _____

❑ 3. **endemic** (line 11) _____

❑ 4. **habitat** (line 12) _____

❑ 5. **encroachment** (line 14) _____

Set Two

an end or halt   to prevent   warm-blooded vertebrate   the study of animals

eating all types of food

❑ 6. **omnivorous** (line 19) _____

❑ 7. **mammal** (line 24) _____

❑ 8. **moratorium** (line 29) _____

❑ 9. **zoology** (line 37) _____

❑ 10. **avert** (line 40) _____

Self-Tests

MyReadingLab Visit Chapter 12: Environmental Science in MyReadingLab to complete the Self-Test activities.

1 Next to each sentence write the vocabulary word that best applies to the meaning of the sentence. Use each word once.

Set One

VOCABULARY LIST

elicit   endemic   mammals   moratorium   zoology

1. They have been ordered to stop dumping waste there. _____

2. Africa has lots of these, including lions, elephants, and zebras. _____

3. Willow is interested in studying animals. _____

4. Only when I mentioned cookies was I able to get a response from my kids. _____

5. The saguaro cactus is found only in the Southwest. _____

VOCABULARY LIST

| habitat | omnivorous | avert | conservationist | encroachment |

6. Orangutans are at home in the forest, swinging from tree to tree. _____

7. We turned away from Main Street minutes before the crane fell. We were lucky to miss the accident. _____

8. Chimpanzees eat leaves, fruit, insects, birds, and small mammals. _____

9. The city has slowly been growing into the hills, and cougars have recently been seen in people's back yards. _____

10. Grandpa belongs to a group that spends two weekends a month removing nonnative plants from local parks. _____

2 Fill in each blank with the appropriate vocabulary word. Use each word once.

VOCABULARY LIST

| avert | endemic | mammal | elicit | conservationist |
| omnivorous | zoology | encroachment | habitats | moratorium |

Henry was surprised that seeing a blue whale would (1)_____ so many emotions from him. He was happy, sad, and amazed. He had been told that they are the world's largest (2)_____ (as long as three school buses), but he hadn't really comprehended that until he saw one in person. He was so impressed that he wanted to do something to (3)_____ their disappearance. It was on that day that Henry became a(n) (4)_____. Now he writes letters, sends money, and works with local groups to preserve the (5)_____ of endangered animals in the forests, grasslands, and oceans around the globe.

One of the endangered animals Henry learned about is the aye-aye. It is a primate that is (6)_____ to Madagascar. It eats fruits, nuts, seeds, and grubs, which makes it (7)_____. Due to (8)_____ of its rain forest habitat, aye-aye have been found more often raiding local villages for food. There is a local superstition that the aye-aye is an omen of evil and that it sneaks into people's homes and kills them with its long middle finger. Because of these beliefs, aye-aye are often killed by locals. The story of the aye-aye fascinated Henry and encouraged him to take a(n) (9)_____ course at his local college. As Henry says, "there should never be a(n) (10)_____ on learning."

3 Use the vocabulary words to complete the following analogies. For more instructions, see Completing Analogies on page 6.

VOCABULARY LIST

avert	endemic	zoology	elicit	omnivorous
habitat	mammal	encroachment	conservationist	moratorium

1. New Orleans : city :: desert : _____
2. new : old :: beginning : _____
3. cook : makes food :: _____ : works to save the environment
4. examine : study :: _____ : prevent
5. oak : tree :: giraffe : _____
6. pots and pans : cooking :: questions : _____ answers
7. elephants and gorillas : large :: raccoons and sharks : _____
8. steering wheel : car :: clearing away trees : _____
9. throw : toss :: _____ : native
10. strong winds : falling branches :: curious about animals : study _____

Word Visions

Identify the two vocabulary words represented in the drawings.

1. _____

2. _____

Word Wise

Collocations

Because the college *adheres to* a strict no-drug policy, anyone caught with illegal drugs on campus will be expelled. (Chapter 11)

The man's mission seemed to be to *impede progress* on the new library; he objected to every aspect of the plan. (Chapter 11)

With an especially hot summer, the city put a *moratorium on* selling fireworks. (Chapter 12)

I tried to *elicit a response* from my husband on what he wanted for dinner, but I should have known better than to ask him during a football game. (Chapter 12)

The city was able to *avert a catastrophe* by quarantining those who were infected with the deadly virus within hours of its discovery. (Chapter 12)

Interactive Exercise

Finish the sentence starters that deal with the environment. The first five include one of the vocabulary words in the starter. For the second five, use each of the following vocabulary words once in your completed sentences: elicit, encroachment, habitat, mammal, and omnivorous.

1. As a conservationist, my greatest concern is _____

   _____

2. To avert a catastrophe in regard to the environment, people _____

   _____

3. There needs to be a moratorium on _____

4. The field of zoology can help to protect the planet by _____

   _____

5. Plants and animals that are endemic _____

6. Animals are fascinating because _____

   _____

7. Many of the animals in Africa _____

8. Plants and animals are endangered _____

   _____

9. One way I can help the planet is _____

10. In the next ten years, I hope to see _____

   _____

HINT

Word Groups

Putting words into related groups can help your mind organize new vocabulary. To create word groups, get a piece of paper, pick a category, and list as many of the vocabulary words as possible whose definitions fit under that heading in a general way. You will, of course, need to know the shades of meaning the more frequently you use a word.

Here is a sample list of vocabulary words that fit the category of "hidden or secret": *imply* (Chapter 2), *clandestine* and *intrigue* (Chapter 3), *covert* (Chapter 8). As you work through the book, look for four other words that could fit this category, and return here to add to the list.

1. _____
2. _____
3. _____
4. _____

A few other categories to consider for the vocabulary words in this text are "free/freedom," "cheat," and "excitement." For a fun and collaborative way to use word groups, see the directions for Category Race in Chapter 15.

Word List

avert
[ə vûrt′]
v. 1. to prevent
2. to turn away or aside

conservationist
[kon′ sər vā′ shə nist]
n. a person who works to save the environment; an environmentalist

elicit
[i lis′ it]
v. to draw or bring out; to obtain

encroachment
[en krōch′ mənt]
n. the act of gradually taking over an area or possessions that belong to someone else; an intrusion

endemic
[en dem′ ik]
adj. natural to a particular area; native

habitat
[hab′ i tat′]
n. 1. the environment where a plant or animal typically lives; surroundings
2. the place where something or someone is usually found

mammal
[mam′ əl]
n. warm-blooded vertebrate (animal with a backbone)

moratorium
[môr′ ə tôr′ ē əm]
n. suspension of an activity; an end or halt

omnivorous
[om niv′ ər əs]
adj. eating all types of food

zoology
[zō ol′ ə jē]
n. the study of animals, including their behavior and development

Words to Watch

Which words would you like to practice with a bit more? Pick 3–5 words to study, and list them below. Write the word and its definition, and compose your own sentence using the word correctly. This extra practice could be the final touch to learning a word.

Word	Definition	Your Sentence
1. _____	_____	_____
_____	_____	_____
2. _____	_____	_____
_____	_____	_____
3. _____	_____	_____
_____	_____	_____
4. _____	_____	_____
_____	_____	_____
5. _____	_____	_____
_____	_____	_____

Chapter 13

Computer Science

Internet Scams

Lesson 3: Staying Safe

As you will be working more on the Internet as this course progresses, this week's lessons examine Internet scams. There have always been those who have found ways to **defraud** others, but the Internet has broadened the potential for cheating people. One person can now reach millions with a few keystrokes. The possibilities for increased dishonesty force all of us to learn how to protect ourselves. Here are a few precautions we will examine this week:

- Find out who you are dealing with. **Spam** is the junk mail of the Internet, but occasionally there will be a message that interests you; however, it is up to you to make sure that the company that sent it is trustworthy. Discover where the company is located; find out if it is even a real company. Ask for information in writing, check with the Better Business Bureau about the company's record, and ask people you trust if they have dealt with the company. It is your responsibility to establish the **credibility** of an online business.

- **Circumspection** is the key word to keeping safe on the Internet. If you get an e-mail from what appears to be your bank, credit card, or other company you do business with requesting personal information, be cautious. Legitimate businesses do not ask for your passwords or other private information via e-mail. Also use care when you are on social networking sites such as Facebook. You may be asked to click on a link that can secretly install malware that can corrupt your computer system, or you may be directed to a survey that asks for your personal data. And don't make your password obvious. Don't use your name, birthday, or part of your Social Security number. To make your password hard to **decipher**, use a combination of letters and numbers, and change your password occasionally.

- Be aware of **phishing** (pronounced like fishing). The goal is to hook a person into giving out personal information to be used for dishonest ends. If an e-mail or other site asks for your address, Social Security number, birth date, or mother's maiden name, be suspicious. With any of these pieces of information, crooks can find out more about you until they have enough to steal your identity. It is essential to establish the **validity** of a Web site because identity theft is growing, and it can be an **ordeal** to clear up mistakes. Crooks have stolen credit card information, racked up thousands of dollars in charges, and ruined a person's credit history. The innocent person may only be made aware that a crime has been committed in his or her name when the police show up at the door.

Many offers on the Web sound great, and though some of them may be honest, most of them fall under the old **adage** "if it sounds too good to be true, it probably is." The lessons this week will make you aware of the types of fraud common to the Internet and present ways to protect yourself. The Web has great potential for information and entertainment, but we must remember that **lax** behavior can be dangerous. →

Predicting

For each set, write the definition on the line next to the word to which it belongs. If you are unsure, return to the reading, and underline any context clues you find. After you've made your predictions, check your answers against the Word List at the end of the chapter. Place a checkmark in the box next to each word whose definition you missed. These are the words you'll want to study closely.

Set One

| watchfulness | to cheat | trustworthiness | junk e-mail | to decode |

- ☐ 1. **defraud** (line 3) _____
- ☐ 2. **spam** (line 9) _____
- ☐ 3. **credibility** (line 13) _____
- ☐ 4. **circumspection** (line 15) _____
- ☐ 5. **decipher** (line 21) _____

Set Two

| authenticity | a traditional saying | a trying experience | careless |

the practice of luring Internet users to a fake Web site to steal personal information

- ☐ 6. **phishing** (line 23) _____
- ☐ 7. **validity** (line 27) _____
- ☐ 8. **ordeal** (line 27) _____
- ☐ 9. **adage** (line 32) _____
- ☐ 10. **lax** (line 34) _____

Self-Tests

MyReadingLab Visit Chapter 13: Computer Science in MyReadingLab to complete the Self-Test activities.

1 Put a T for true or F for false next to each sentence.

_____ 1. Those involved in phishing are honest people.

_____ 2. It is easy for most people to decipher hieroglyphics.

_____ 3. Planning a wedding can be an ordeal.

_____ 4. Most people like getting spam in their e-mail.

_____ 5. A mechanic should be lax when repairing a car.

_____ 6. When planning a surprise party, it can be helpful to use circumspection.

_____ 7. If a couple is going to buy diamonds, they should research the credibility of a store before making a purchase.

_____ 8. It is important to check the validity of a medicine's claims before taking it.

_____ 9. Most parents try to defraud their children out of their allowances.

_____ 10. The adage "The early bird catches the worm" would appeal to most late sleepers.

2 Answer the following questions using the vocabulary words. Use each word once.

1. Yoon got a virus on his computer. What was his approach to security? _____

2. If a person offers to sell you a new car for two hundred dollars, what can you assume the person is trying to do to you? _____

3. Zora couldn't read the note from her brother because he had written it as he hurried out the door. What couldn't she do? _____

4. Toshi carefully read the contract when he signed with a baseball team. What did he want to check? _____

5. What is "The bigger they are, the harder they fall"? _____

6. What would most people call spending a night on the floor of an airport and not having eaten for sixteen hours? _____

7. When trying to find the appropriate birthday present, Fern carefully asked around about some of Juanita's favorite things. What was Fern using? _____

8. Herschel examined several investment firms before giving one his money. What did he want to determine about each company? _____

9. If you get an e-mail that appears to be from your credit card company but asks for your password, what is someone doing? _____

10. The company sent out millions of e-mails to announce their new product. What did they do to people? _____

3 Complete the sentences using the vocabulary words. Use each word once.

VOCABULARY LIST

spam	validity	phishing	ordeal	decipher
lax	adage	defraud	credibility	circumspection

1. People try to _____ others by stealing their credit card numbers.

2. A detective needs to use _____ when he or she is following someone.

3. The _____ of the witness was called into question when it was discovered the man had been engaged to the suspect in college. It wasn't clear whether he still loved her.

4. I write my notes neatly so I can _____ them when studying for an exam.

5. Traveling to see my uncle is a(n) _____ in the winter; he lives on a dirt road, and it becomes a huge mud pit after even a little rain.

6. I thought I was being careful, but I became a victim of _____. I gave out my Social Security number on a Web site that I thought belonged to my bank.

7. I hate getting _____ in my inbox. I have to delete three to four junk messages each day.

8. Upon learning that the couple had not correctly filled out the marriage license, lawyers had to be contacted to confirm the _____ of the marriage.

9. My _____ study habits caused me to fail two of my midterms. I wasn't as careless the rest of the term.

10. I agree with the _____ "Don't count your chickens before they're hatched." You can never be sure about a situation until it is over.

Identify the two vocabulary words represented in the photos.

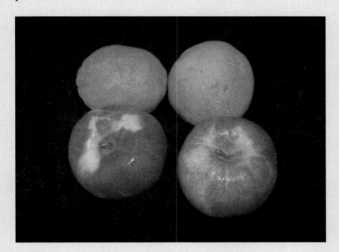

1. _____

2. _____

Word Wise

Collocations

I should have heeded the *old adage* "Look before you leap," but I joined the soccer team before realizing how hard the training was or how often I would have to practice. (Chapter 13)

I got careless and failed to check the *validity of* a Web site sent to me in an e-mail. I thought the e-mail was from a friend, but it turned out to be from a company that had hijacked her contact list. (Chapter 13)

Bonnie could not *face the ordeal* of another Thanksgiving at her aunt's house; ten screaming children and eleven cats were too much for her to take. (Chapter 13)

Interesting Etymologies

Ordeal (Chapter 13) comes from a medieval form of trial. If a court could not decide a person's guilt or innocence using the evidence presented, the person had to undergo an *ordal*, meaning "judgment." The person was subjected to a cruel physical test such as putting one's hand in boiling water. If the person showed no injuries after three days, he or she was found innocent. Today an ordeal is "a harsh or trying test or experience," but it is no longer forced on one by the courts.

Spam (Chapter 13) as a food product got its name in 1937 from its main ingredient "sp(iced) (h)am." The meaning of "junk e-mail" came in the early 1990s. It is likely taken from a skit done on the British television series *Monty Python's Flying Circus* (1970s) where a restaurant's menu extensively features the food product Spam. In the skit, the word *spam* is repeated continuously, just as spam is sent again and again.

Interactive Exercise

Answer the following questions about computers and the Internet.

1. What is one way you can check the validity of a Web site?

_____

2. What are two items that are frequently offered in spam?

_____

_____

3. What kind of statement would you want to check the credibility of before you considered buying a product advertised online?

_____

4. When you first started using a computer, did you find it an ordeal or a pleasure? Explain why.

_____

_____

5. Think of a situation when circumspection would be especially important to use on the Internet.

_____

6. What can you do to protect yourself from phishing?

_____

7. What is one way someone might try to defraud you on the Internet?

_____

8. What is one reason a person shouldn't be lax when on the Internet?

_____

9. Do you find it hard to decipher instructions when you do something on the computer? Give an example of a time it was difficult, or explain why you don't have problems with computers.

_____

_____

10. What is an adage that could apply to using computers?

_____

Conversation Starters

An excellent way to review the vocabulary words and help to make them your own is to use them when you are speaking. Gather three to five friends or classmates, and use one or more of the conversation starters below. Before you begin talking, have each person write down six of the vocabulary words he or she will use during the conversation. Share your lists with each other to check that you did not all pick the same six words. Try to cover all of the words you want to study, whether you are reviewing one, two, or more chapters.

1. What was a memorable early experience you had with reading? How did you get access to books?
2. What steps can people take to protect endangered animals?
3. In what ways do you use the Internet? How do you protect your personal information?

Word List

adage
[ad′ ij]
    n. a traditional saying;
    a proverb

circumspection
[sûr′ kəm spek′ shən]
    n. watchfulness; caution; care

credibility
[kred′ ə bil′ ə tē]
    n. trustworthiness; believability

decipher
[di sī′ fər]
    v. to decode; to make out;
    to make sense of

defraud
[di frôd′]
    v. to take away a right, money,
    or property by deception;
    to cheat

lax
[laks]
    adj. not strict; careless; loose

ordeal
[ôr dēl′, ôr′ dēl]
    n. a harsh or trying test
    or experience

phishing
[fish′ ing]
    n. the practice of luring
    innocent Internet users to a
    fake Web site by using real-
    looking e-mail with the goal
    to steal personal information
    or introduce a virus

spam
[spam]
    n. junk e-mail, often advertis-
    ing, sent to multiple
    individuals

    v. 1. to send unwanted e-mail
       2. to send to multiple
       individuals

With a capital "S"

    n. a canned meat product
    made mainly from pork

validity
[və lid′ i tē]
    n. 1. authenticity; legal
       soundness
       2. strength; authority

Words to Watch

Which words would you like to practice with a bit more? Pick 3–5 words to study, and list them below. Write the word and its definition, and compose your own sentence using the word correctly. This extra practice could be the final touch to learning a word.

Word	Definition	Your Sentence
1. _____	_____	_____
2. _____	_____	_____
3. _____	_____	_____
4. _____	_____	_____
5. _____	_____	_____

Chapter 14

Word Parts III

Look for words with these **prefixes, roots,** and/or **suffixes** as you work through this book. You may have already seen some of them, and you will see others in later chapters. Learning basic word parts can help you figure out the meanings of unfamiliar words.

prefix: a word part added to the beginning of a word that changes the meaning of the root

root: a word's basic part with its essential meaning

suffix: a word part added to the end of a word; indicates the part of speech

Word Part	Meaning	Examples and Definitions
Prefixes		
anti-	against	*antipathy:* dislike; a feeling against *antidote:* a remedy given to act against a poison
circum-	around, on all sides	*circumnavigate:* to sail around *circumspect:* watchful; looking around
pan-	all, everywhere	*pandemonium:* disorder everywhere *panorama:* an all-around view
Roots		
-don-, -dot-, -dow-	give	*donate:* to give away *antidote:* a remedy given to cure something
-fer-	bring, carry	*transfer:* to carry across *offer:* to volunteer to bring
-hab-, -hib-	hold	*habitat:* the environment that holds a plant or animal *inhibition:* the act of holding back
-ven-, -vent-	come, move toward	*convene:* to come together *adventurous:* inclined to move toward new experiences
-voc-, -vok-	call	*provocative:* calling attention to *invoke:* to call on for support
Suffixes		
-ia (makes a noun)	condition	*euphoria:* a condition of extreme happiness *insomnia:* the condition of being unable to sleep
-ology (makes a noun)	the study of	*zoology:* the study of animals *biology:* the study of life

Self-Tests

MyReadingLab Visit Chapter 14: Word Parts III in MyReadingLab to complete the Self-Test activities.

1 Read each definition and choose the appropriate word from the list below. Use each word once. The meaning of the word part is underlined to help you make the connection. Refer to the Word Parts list if you need help.

VOCABULARY LIST

prohibit	intervene	astrology	donor	antiwar
circumvent	advocate	inertia	conference	panorama

1. someone who <u>gives</u> something _____
2. to put a <u>hold</u> on doing _____
3. to avoid by moving <u>around</u> _____
4. to <u>come</u> between _____
5. an <u>all</u>-around view _____
6. a person who <u>calls</u> for the support of a cause _____
7. the <u>condition</u> of not moving _____
8. a meeting that <u>brings</u> people together _____
9. <u>the study of</u> the stars as influences on people's lives _____
10. <u>against</u> combat _____

2 Finish the sentences with the meaning of each word part. Use each meaning once. The word part is underlined to help you make the connection.

VOCABULARY LIST

give	against	come	bring	the study of
condition	call	all	around	hold

1. It could pro<u>voke</u> a fight if you _____ someone a liar.
2. My mother uses a hug as a <u>pan</u>acea, a cure for _____ problems, and it often works.
3. Matthew is going to _____ a large en<u>dow</u>ment to the local art museum because he has always wanted to be a painter.
4. To understand the reading, I had to in<u>fer</u> what the author meant, or _____ out his meaning.
5. If you <u>circum</u>navigate the globe, you sail _____ it.
6. I will pursue _____ psy<u>cho</u>logy because I enjoy learning about the mind.
7. An <u>anti</u>-aging cream is meant to work _____ getting older.
8. My nail-biting <u>hab</u>it has such a _____ on me that I am going to seek professional help to stop it.
9. Carol's no<u>stalg</u>ia for home was a _____ we were able to treat by cooking a few of her favorite Southern dishes.
10. Everyone wants to _____ to the e<u>vent</u> at the stadium, but only people who bought tickets a month ago can get in.

3 Finish the story using the word parts below. Use each word part once. Your knowledge of word parts, as well as the context clues, will help you create the correct words. If you do not understand the meaning of a word you have made, check your dictionary for the definition or to see whether the word exists.

WORD PARTS

| circum | anti | don | fer | ven | ia | ology | pan | hib | vok |

Helping a Friend

I of(1)_____ed to take care of my friend's cat for a week while she went to a conference. She is a doctor, and every year she goes to a dermat(2)_____ conference to learn more about skin care. Due to some (3)_____stances that she didn't make clear, her regular sitter wasn't available. She told me her cat was really amiable and that I would love spending time with him. I adore cats, and I was thinking about getting one myself, so I thought this would be a good opportunity to test my pet skills. I said to drop him by on Friday whenever it was con(4)_____ient for her.

I was surprised when I saw BW. My friend had described him as fragile, but he ex(5)_____ited every sign of being a hardy animal. She handed me a list of when he should eat, what he should eat, and how much he should eat. She told me she didn't con(6)_____e his scratching any furniture, so I was supposed to spray him with water if he tried to do so. My excitement of having a pet for a week was rapidly turning to (7)_____pathy as she continued with her long list of instructions. It was, however, too late to re(8)_____e my offer.

After two days, my friend called me terribly upset. I had to talk to her for ten minutes to quiet her hyster(9)_____. Finally, I understood that she had had a dream that my house was filled with (10)_____demonium and that poor BW was upset. I told her everything was calm and that he had just been sitting on my lap while I read. I assured her that we were getting along exceedingly well. She insisted that she couldn't relax until I sent photos showing that BW was all right. I e-mailed her a few photos and swore it was the last time I'd cat-sit for her.

4 Pick the best definition for each underlined word using your knowledge of word parts. Circle the word part in each of the underlined words.

a. condition of being afraid

b. coming

c. the study of birds

d. distance around

e. to bring on rapidly

f. money or property given by a bride to her husband

g. a temple to all gods

h. holding back

i. a calling; a career

j. against being with others

_____ 1. My mom says I am <u>antisocial</u>, but I really enjoy having time alone on the weekends.

_____ 2. The <u>circumference</u> of the circle was hard to figure out because I forgot the formula.

_____ 3. While in Greece we visited the remains of a <u>pantheon</u> with statues of Athena, Zeus, and other gods.

_____ 4. The <u>advent</u> of the holiday season caused me to sit down and make some plans.

_____ 5. Diana's <u>dowry</u> was considerable: a castle in England and $100,000.

_____ 6. I am certain nursing is the right <u>vocation</u> for me.

_____ 7. The offers for starring roles began to <u>proliferate</u> after Arturo won an Oscar.

_____ 8. The lack of children's books in the library is <u>inhibiting</u> the students' learning. By fourth grade most of the students have read every book in the junior section.

_____ 9. I didn't know Mai had a <u>phobia</u> of flowers until she refused to enter the florist shop.

_____ 10. After a fascinating day of observing condors, vultures, and falcons at the zoo, I may have a future in <u>ornithology</u>.

5 A good way to remember word parts is to pick one word that uses a word part and understand how that word part functions in the word. Then you can apply that meaning to other words that have the same word part. Use the following words to help you match the word part to its meaning.

Set One

_____ 1. **circum-:** circumnavigate, circumvent, circumstances

_____ 2. **-ia:** insomnia, nostalgia, euphoria

_____ 3. **anti-:** antipathy, antisocial, antidote

_____ 4. **-don-, -dot-, -dow-:** donate, antidote, endow

_____ 5. **-fer-:** transfer, proliferate, confer

a. against

b. give

c. condition

d. around, on all sides

e. bring, carry

Set Two

_____ 6. **-ven-, -vent-:** convene, intervene, advent

_____ 7. **-voc-, -vok-:** provocative, advocate, invoke

_____ 8. **-ology:** zoology, biology, psychology

_____ 9. **-hab-, -hib-:** habitat, inhibition, prohibit

_____ 10. **pan-:** pandemonium, panoramic, pantheon

f. hold

g. all, everywhere

h. call

i. come, move toward

j. the study of

Interactive Exercise

Use the dictionary to find a word you don't know that uses each word part listed below. Write the meaning of the word part, the word, and the definition. If your dictionary has the etymology (history) of the word, see how the word part relates to the meaning, and write the etymology after the definition.

Word Part	Meaning	Word	Definition and Etymology
EXAMPLE:			
-ven-	come, move toward	venue	the place where an event happens; Latin "venire," to come
1. *anti-*			
2. *circum-*			
3. *pan-*			
4. *-don-*			
5. *-fer-*			

Word Wise

Internet Activity: For Further Study

When you get the urge to expand your vocabulary knowledge online, try visiting the sites below.

- For a list of challenging words, several of which you are learning in this text, and how many times a word has appeared in the *New York Times* in the last year with an example of the word in context, visit learning.blogs.nytimes.com/category/word-of-the-day.
- For dictionary entries, a word-of-the-day feature, and word-related games, give the Merriam-Webster online dictionary a look at m-w.com.
- To see a video of the Spam skit mentioned in Chapter 13, visit youtube.com. While you are there, type in a few vocabulary words (e.g., mammal or claustrophobia) to see other videos related to the words.

Enjoy exploring the Internet's many resources, but remember to watch your time online.

Match each photograph to one of the word parts below, and write the meaning of the word part.

anti-   pan-   -don-/-dot-/-dow-   -hab-/-hib-   -ia

1. _____

2. _____

HINT

Marking Words When Reading

When you read for fun, it can be counterproductive to stop and look up every word you don't know—you will become frustrated with reading instead of enjoying it. As this book advocates, looking for context clues is the best way to find the meaning of an unknown word, but sometimes this method doesn't work. There are various ways of keeping track of unfamiliar words; try these methods to see which fits your style.

- Keep a piece of paper and a pen next to you, and write down the word and page number.
- Keep a piece of paper next to you, and rip it into small pieces or use sticky notes. Put a piece between the pages where the word you don't know is located. For added help, write the word on the paper.
- If the book belongs to you, circle the words you don't know and flip through the book later to find them.
- If the book belongs to you, dog-ear the page (turn the corner down) where the word you don't know is located. This method is useful when you don't have paper or a pen handy.
- Repeat the word and page number to yourself a few times. Try to connect the page number to a date to help you remember it.

When you are done reading for the day, get your dictionary and look up the words you marked. The last two methods work best if you don't read many pages before you look up the words or if there are only a few words you don't know. Using these methods will help you learn new words without damaging the fun of reading. Note: If you come across a word you don't know several times and not knowing its meaning hinders your understanding of what is going on, then it's a good idea to stop and look up the word.

Chapter 15

Review

Focus on Chapters 11–14

The following activities give you the opportunity to further interact with the vocabulary words you've been learning. By taking tests, answering questions, using visuals, doing a crossword puzzle, and working with others, you will see which words you know well and which ones need additional study.

Self-Tests MyReadingLab Visit Chapter 15: Review in MyReadingLab to complete the Self-Test activities.

LO 4,8 **1** Match each term with its synonym in Set One and its antonym in Set Two.

Synonyms

Set One

_____ 1. impose   a. end

_____ 2. decipher   b. decode

_____ 3. defraud   c. assist

_____ 4. moratorium   d. force

_____ 5. facilitate   e. cheat

Antonyms

Set Two

_____ 6. advocate   f. firm

_____ 7. lax   g. retreat

_____ 8. circumspection   h. opponent

_____ 9. impede   i. assist

_____ 10. encroachment   j. carelessness

Remember to add words to Word Reactions on page 175 after completing the Review chapter activities.

2 Pick the word that best completes each sentence.

1. Whenever I hear the _____ "A stitch in time saves nine," I think about the time I didn't fix my leaky sink right away and ended up having to repair my whole bathroom floor.

   a. moratorium   b. habitat   c. adage   d. potential

2. Brown bears are _____ animals who feast on berries and salmon.

   a. susceptible   b. omnivorous   c. potential   d. endemic

3. Gianna was _____ to silly suggestions, so it wasn't surprising when she wore her pajamas to the opera.

   a. lax   b. omnivorous   c. susceptible   d. innate

4. The unusual-looking platypus is _____ to Australia.

   a. innate   b. lax   c. endemic   d. susceptible

5. Fraud is a huge problem on the Internet. Users need to be especially aware of Web sites that look real but are used for _____.

   a. phishing   b. nurture   c. zoology   d. encroachment

6. Zebras are one of my favorite _____ because of their black and white coloring.

   a. habitats   b. ordeals   c. advocates   d. mammals

7. Pessimism seems to be a(n) _____ quality in Gus. Even as a child, I rarely saw him cheerful.

   a. lax   b. innate   c. endemic   d. susceptible

8. I would never respond to _____ related to medicine. Who knows what I would get if I ordered medicine online from an unknown company.

   a. spam   b. nurture   c. credibility   d. encroachment

LO 1 **3** Pick the vocabulary word that best completes the sentence. Use each word once.

nurture	facilitate	elicit	defraud	avert

1. If your forms and receipts are organized, it will _____ our preparing your tax return.

2. The doctor tried to _____ a response from the patient, but he was too dazed to answer her.

3. I believe that it is important to _____ a love of nature in children, so I take my kids to the park, beach, or mountains every week.

4. We were able to _____ a catastrophe when Keri grabbed Jimmy just before the pan filled with hot oil was about to fall on him.

5. When the boy tried to _____ his neighbor by saying he had mowed her lawn every week, she fired him. She knew he had only been by once that month.

4 Complete the following sentences that illustrate collocations. The rest of the collocation is in italics. Use each word or phrase once.

to	on	face the	of	a response	progress

1. It is important to check the *validity* _____ a Web site before you use the information on it in a research paper.

2. The school put a *moratorium* _____ cell phone use because students were texting during classes.

3. Constant arguing at City Hall continues to *impede* _____ on the plans to redevelop downtown.

4. Ernesto *adheres* _____ a strict study plan of an hour every day from four to five in the afternoon.

5. I pounded on the door, rang the doorbell a dozen times, and shouted for ten minutes, but I couldn't *elicit* _____ from anyone in the house.

6. After forty job interviews, I am uncertain whether I can _____ *ordeal* of another one.

5 Fill in the missing meaning for the underlined word part.

around	hold	the study of	call	believe	all
a person who	turn				

1. The <u>habit</u>at of the koala bear has to _____ eucalyptus trees because the animals eat the leaves of the trees and live in the branches.

2. I had to a<u>vert</u> my eyes when I saw my daughter hiding "treasures" around the living room for me to find. I decided to _____ around and head back to the kitchen until she called me to play.

3. I consider myself a conservation<u>ist</u>; I am _____ cares about the environment and works to protect it.

4. I am an ad<u>voc</u>ate for smaller class sizes in elementary schools. I regularly _____ members of local and state political groups and let them know why it is an important issue.

5. I thought it wise to use <u>circum</u>spection when I spoke about marriage. I wanted to be careful _____ the topic because Leena and her husband are having problems with their marriage.

6. I love my zo<u>ology</u> class. I am finding _____ animals to be a fascinating subject.

7. It seems to me that <u>omni</u>vorous animals have a better chance of survival since they can eat _____ kinds of food, not just meat or vegetables.

8. The man's <u>cred</u>ibility was called into question when he said he lived in Florida, but it was hard to _____ him when he didn't know that Tallahassee is the capital.

LO 1 **6** Finish the story using the vocabulary words below. Use each word once.

VOCABULARY LIST

surpass   lax   credibility   nurture   ordeal

zoology   potential   innate   habitat   decipher

In South America

I was excited when my parents announced that
we were taking a trip to Chile and Peru. They said
they felt I had the (1)_____ to be
an archaeologist or historian. They wanted to
(2)_____ my interests in both areas by
exposing me to ancient cultures and historic sites. My
usual summer (3)_____ was the couch in
front of the television, so this was going to be an exciting adventure. My parents had carefully checked out
the (4)_____ of the tour operator, so we
knew our travel arrangements would be handled well.
I had been (5)_____ with my Spanish
lessons in high school, so I was a bit confused when

we got to the airport in Santiago, Chile. I was, however, able to (6)_____ the departure
board and find our flight to the Atacama Desert. I was also able to order us each a café con leche.

We live on the coast in Oregon, so I was excited to see the desert. Parts of the Atacama Desert
have never received recorded rainfall. It is the driest desert in the world. One of our day trips was to
the geysers at El Tatio. To avert any possible effects of altitude sickness (we would be at 14,000 feet),
we ate a light dinner the evening before the trip. The biggest (7)_____ of the whole
vacation for me was getting up at 4 a.m. and then trying to catch more sleep on the bumpy ride to the
geysers. We arrived at 7 a.m., which our guide said was the best time to see the geysers. On the way
back, we saw flamingos, llamas, and a beautiful guanaco. I was especially thrilled to see the guanaco.
While I was admiring it, my mother remembered that I had a(n) (8)_____ skill with
animals. As a kid, I befriended every dog and cat in our neighborhood. My parents decided to add
(9)_____ to the areas I might major in.

I didn't think it was possible but the trip went on to (10)_____ my expectations.
Other highlights were seeing the remains of mummified people, visiting the poet Pablo Neruda's
house, and exploring the ruins at Machu Picchu. It was a summer filled with adventure. And my
parents were right: the trip did develop in me a desire to study archaeology, though I haven't ruled out
zoology.

Interactive Exercise

Answer the following questions to further test your understanding of the vocabulary words.

1. What is one thing society should put a moratorium on?

   _____

2. List four foods that would illustrate what an omnivorous person might eat.

   _____

   _____

3. What can you do to surpass your goals for a course?

   _____

   _____

4. What would a friend have to do to destroy his or her credibility with you?

   _____

   _____

5. How are people susceptible to weather conditions? Give two examples.

   _____

   _____

6. Name two mammals you like.

   _____

   _____

7. What is one way you can protect yourself from phishing?

   _____

   _____

8. Where might you find people who adhere to the belief of nature's soothing powers? Provide three examples.

   _____

   _____

9. What are two rules your parents imposed on you as a child?

   _____

   _____

10. What would you want to check the validity of before making a decision on whether to buy it or to take action on it?

    _____

    _____

LO 6 **Person, Place, or Thing**

Use the three photos to write two sentences about
each person, place, and thing. Use at least one of the
vocabulary words below in each sentence. In total,
you will use at least six different vocabulary words from the list.

VOCABULARY LIST

adhere	impose	nurture	potential	surpass
avert	conservationist	encroachment	endemic	mammal
adage	defraud	lax	spam	validity

1. _____

2. _____

3. _____

4. _____

5. _____

6. _____

Crossword Puzzle LO 3

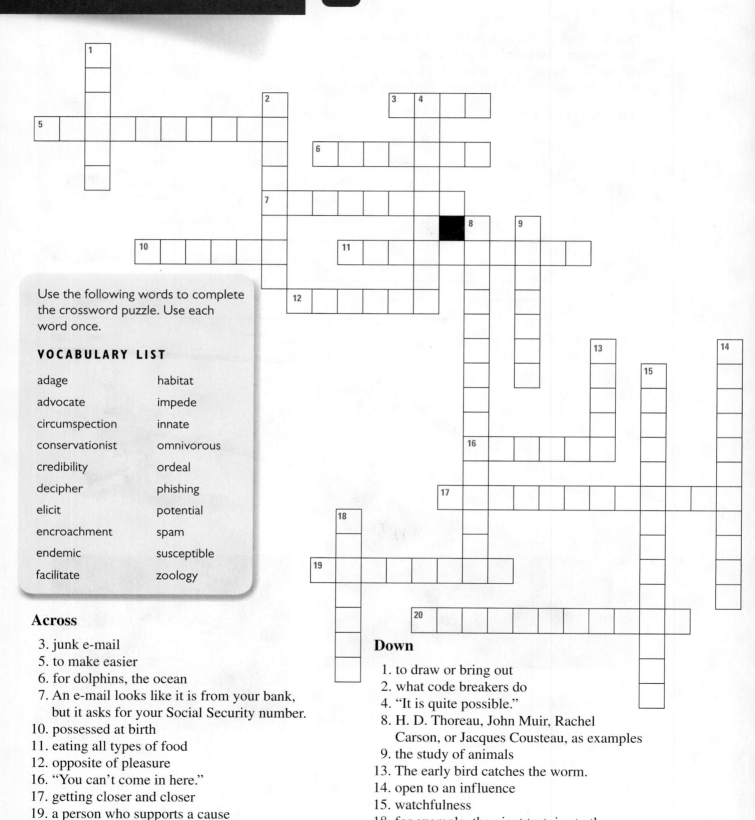

Use the following words to complete the crossword puzzle. Use each word once.

VOCABULARY LIST

adage	habitat
advocate	impede
circumspection	innate
conservationist	omnivorous
credibility	ordeal
decipher	phishing
elicit	potential
encroachment	spam
endemic	susceptible
facilitate	zoology

Across

3. junk e-mail
5. to make easier
6. for dolphins, the ocean
7. An e-mail looks like it is from your bank, but it asks for your Social Security number.
10. possessed at birth
11. eating all types of food
12. opposite of pleasure
16. "You can't come in here."
17. getting closer and closer
19. a person who supports a cause
20. believability

Down

1. to draw or bring out
2. what code breakers do
4. "It is quite possible."
8. H. D. Thoreau, John Muir, Rachel Carson, or Jacques Cousteau, as examples
9. the study of animals
13. The early bird catches the worm.
14. open to an influence
15. watchfulness
18. for example, the giant tortoise to the Galapagos Islands

HINT

Test-Taking Strategies

Of course, studying is essential to do well on a test, but for some people that isn't enough to ease the stress that testing can bring. A few strategies may help you deal with test anxiety. A healthy body leads to a good test-taking experience, so get a good night's rest, and eat a healthy breakfast, lunch, or dinner before the exam. Exercise before the exam. Take a walk or do some stretching to help you relax. When you get to the classroom, take a few deep breaths and visualize yourself in a soothing spot such as hiking in a forest or floating in a pool. Also picture yourself as being successful at the test; don't focus on any negatives. Being a bit nervous can help during a test by keeping you alert, but too much stress can ruin even the most prepared student's chances of success. If test anxiety becomes a serious problem for you, contact your college's counseling center for advice.

Mix It Up LO 4,7,8

Category Race

Get together with a dozen classmates or so and form three to four teams. Each team needs a set of flash cards for the words to be studied and a blank sheet of paper. Each team thinks of a category, writes it on the top of the sheet of paper, and places flash cards that fit in that category underneath the heading. Alternatively, you can write the words on the paper. After ten minutes, call time. Each group reads its category and words aloud. There may be some disagreement on whether a word fits the category; discuss the word and its meanings to decide these issues. The team that supplies the most words wins. Another way to play is to give each team the same category and seven minutes to record its words. You can also do this activity with each person making his or her own category list. If you do it individually, you can compete with just three or four people.

Possible categories:

1. travel
2. sports
3. health
4. history
5. love life
6. politics
7. business
8. undesirable qualities

Sample sheet:

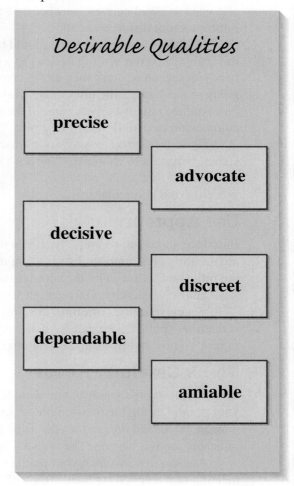

Chapter 16

English

Writing Tips

When writing for school, work, or personal use, here are a few points to keep in mind that will make your writing more effective and interesting.

Generally Avoid

5   The **euphemism**, **cliché**, and **colloquialism** are best avoided in formal writing. Euphemisms are replacement words used for terms that are considered unpleasant. You may have heard a small house called cozy by a real-estate agent or "passed away" used to describe the sad situation of death. You usu-
10   ally want to avoid euphemisms because they tend to hide information or distort a situation.

Clichés, overused phrases, should be avoided because they can make your writing as dead as a doornail. They are handy in speech because they easily convey an idea: "I'm
15   going to sleep like a log after today's hike." In writing, however, they are usually boring. Make your writing more engaging by creating your own original comparison or plainly state your point: "I'm exhausted."

Colloquialisms are words or phrases used in everyday speech that usually aren't appropriate in formal writing. For example, "She ain't interested in goin' to the movie with us" uses two colloquial-
20   isms: "ain't" for "isn't" and "goin'" for "going." Unless your goal is to capture the flavor of everyday speech, avoid colloquialisms.

Use Appropriately

Introduce an **acronym** properly. If you refer to a CD, your readers may initially be **bewildered** if they are thinking of a compact disc and you mean a certificate of deposit. To use an acronym, first write
25   the full name followed by the acronym in parentheses: British Broadcasting Corporation (BBC). Now you can use the acronym throughout your paper, and the reader will know what you are referring to.

Watch your use of **homonyms**. Pay attention when you use words that sound alike, and are sometimes spelled alike, but have different meanings, such as which and witch. **Scrutinize** your writing for homonym errors, and if you often mix up certain homonyms, carefully proofread for those.

30   ### Think Carefully About

Consider the words you use; you want to be **concise** while still giving enough information to convey your point. During the revision phase, look for wordiness. For example, in "Mary is a loud and noisy woman," *loud* and *noisy* mean the same thing, so only one of the words is needed, and Mary's name indicates she is a woman. The revised "Mary is loud" is more powerful.

35   Also learn how much your reader wants you to cover. Does your boss want a **synopsis** of the meeting or a detailed account? You will likely not appreciate the **irony** when you have stayed up all night writing a ten-page report on a sales call to find your boss the next day praising the 200-word summary a colleague wrote in half an hour.

Predicting

For each set, write the definition on the line next to the word to which it belongs. If you are unsure, return to the reading, and underline any context clues you find. After you've made your predictions, check your answers against the Word List at the end of the chapter. Place a checkmark in the box next to each word whose definition you missed. These are the words you'll want to study closely.

Set One

> a commonplace expression   a mild expression substituted for one considered harsh
>
> a word or abbreviation formed from initial letters   an expression used in informal language   confused

❏ 1. **euphemism** (line 5) _____

❏ 2. **cliché** (line 5) _____

❏ 3. **colloquialism** (line 5) _____

❏ 4. **acronym** (line 23) _____

❏ 5. **bewildered** (line 23) _____

Set Two

> brief   two or more words that have the same sound but differ in meaning   a summary
>
> to examine carefully   a clash between what is expected to happen and what really does

❏ 6. **homonyms** (line 27) _____

❏ 7. **scrutinize** (line 28) _____

❏ 8. **concise** (line 31) _____

❏ 9. **synopsis** (line 35) _____

❏ 10. **irony** (line 36) _____

Self-Tests

> **MyReadingLab** Visit Chapter 16: English in MyReadingLab to complete the Self-Test activities.

1 Circle the correct word to complete each sentence.

1. When writing you should avoid using (clichés, acronyms) because they make your writing as dull as dirt.

2. I gave the judge a (concise, cliché) history of my problems with the store; I thought all the details would bore him.

3. I gave my friend a (colloquialism, synopsis) of a five-hundred-page book in two minutes.

4. Computers have introduced several new (acronyms, colloquialisms) into our language, such as HTML and URL.

5. My cousin always departs using the (euphemism, colloquialism) "outta here."

6. The (irony, synopsis) was obvious when my brother said, "Beautiful day for a picnic," as we looked out at the rain-soaked street.

7. I always (bewilder, scrutinize) my credit card bill each month to make sure I haven't been overcharged.

8. It is important to be aware of (homonyms, euphemisms) because they can be used to mislead people; for example, instead of going to war, a country may be involved in "a military action."

9. I was (scrutinized, bewildered) by my son's note that he was going to pick up his dad at the airport. His dad was out front mowing the lawn.

10. It is important to double-check your writing for (homonym, irony) errors, such as *their, there,* and *they're.*

Word Visions

Identify the two vocabulary words represented in the photos.

1. _____

2. _____

2 Put a T for true or F for false next to each sentence.

_____ 1. Acronyms are popular with computer users.

_____ 2. "Cool as a cucumber" is a cliché.

_____ 3. Fair (a carnival) and fair (reasonable) are homonyms.

_____ 4. Knowing the best way to get to the museum would show that the person is bewildered.

_____ 5. If it is snowing and your friend says, "It sure is cold," his statement is an example of irony.

_____ 6. "Powder room" and "comfort station" could be considered euphemisms for the bathroom.

_____ 7. It is a good idea to use colloquialisms in your college papers.

_____ 8. Talking to your friend for three hours about last night's date would be giving her a concise version.

_____ 9. When your boss looks over your five-page report in two minutes, he has really scrutinized it.

_____ 10. A synopsis of an article should take less time to read than the original.

3 Match each word below to the appropriate example.

VOCABULARY LIST

| acronyms | homonyms | bewilder | synopsis | clichés |
| concise | euphemisms | irony | scrutinize | colloquialism |

1. I see that this hem you just sewed is missing three stitches. _____

2. I thought my friends were planning a surprise party for me; instead, they completely forgot my birthday. _____

3. patience and patients _____

4. I could go for a hamburger for lunch. _____

5. "Tell me about the party." "It was a huge success." _____

6. fit for a king, the greatest thing since sliced bread _____

7. let go, dismissed, made redundant, outplaced _____

8. ATM, NASA, ASAP, WWW _____

9. The story is about a girl who goes to a house and tries three bowls of porridge. One is too hot, one is too cold, and the other is just right. While she is napping, the bears that live in the house come home, and she runs away. _____

10. Why are there golf balls all over the kitchen floor? _____

Word Wise

Context Clue Mini-Lesson 4

This lesson uses the general meaning of a sentence or passage to help you understand the meaning of the underlined words. In the paragraph below, circle any words that give you clues to the meaning. Then write your own definitions of the underlined words on the lines next to the words that follow the paragraph.

Though I only heard a <u>snippet</u> of my parents' conversation as I walked past their room, it was enough for me to know that I had to leave. They always tried to <u>coddle</u> me, but I was ready to go away to college, and they weren't going to stop me. I would <u>spurn</u> their offer to pay for all of my college expenses if I stayed at home. Though the route to my independence might be <u>tortuous</u>, I was willing to face the challenges to show my parents that I was becoming an adult. I would apply to colleges across the country and look for a job tomorrow.

Your Definition

1. Snippet _____

2. Coddle _____

3. Spurn _____

4. Tortuous _____

Interactive Exercise

Practice using the vocabulary words by completing the following activities.

1. What are two acronyms used on your campus?

   _____

   _____

2. Name something that bewilders you.

   _____

3. List two sets of homonyms you often use.

   _____

   _____

4. What does the cliché "We'll cross that bridge when we come to it" mean? Does it seem like a smart way of thinking? Explain why you feel it is or isn't.

   _____

   _____

5. Give an example of a colloquialism you often use or that you hear used.

   _____

6. Euphemisms are popular for "used" items, such as the term *preowned automobile.* List two other euphemisms for used goods.

   _____

7. List two things you would want to scrutinize before buying.

   _____

8. Write a synopsis of a movie you like.

   _____

   _____

   _____

9. Give an example of a statement you might make to a friend that would show irony.

   _____

10. Give a concise recounting of your activities yesterday.

    _____

    _____

HINT

A World of Words

Keep your eyes open for new words. You will certainly encounter new words in the textbooks you read and in the lectures your professors give, but new words can be found everywhere. Don't turn off your learning when you leave the classroom. When you see a new word in the newspaper, on the Internet, or any other place, use the strategies you have learned in this book: Look for context clues around the new word, try to predict the meaning, and check the dictionary if you aren't sure of the meaning. No matter where you are or how old you may be, your vocabulary can continue to grow.

Word List

acronym
[ak′rə nim′]
n. a word or abbreviation formed from the initial letters or groups of letters of the words in a name or phrase

bewilder
[bi wil′ dər]
v. to confuse, baffle, or puzzle

cliché
[klē shā′]
n. a commonplace or over-used expression or idea

colloquialism
[kə lō′ kwē ə liz′ əm]
n. an expression used in conversational or informal language, not usually appropriate for formal writing

concise
[kən sīs′]
adj. expressing much in a few words; brief

euphemism
[yōō′ fə miz′ əm]
n. a mild or vague expression substituted for one considered harsh

homonym
[hom′ ə nim′, hō′ mə-]
n. one of two or more words that have the same sound and sometimes the same spelling but differ in meaning

irony
[ī′ rə nē, ī′ ər-]
n. 1. a clash between what is expected to happen and what really does, often used humorously in literature
2. the use of words to state the opposite of their precise meaning

scrutinize
[skrōōt′ n īz]
v. to examine carefully, especially looking for errors; to inspect

synopsis
[si nop′ sis]
n. a brief statement that gives a general idea; a summary

Words to Watch

Which words would you like to practice with a bit more? Pick 3–5 words to study, and list them below. Write the word and its definition, and compose your own sentence using the word correctly. This extra practice could be the final touch to learning a word.

Word	Definition	Your Sentence
1.		
2.		
3.		
4.		
5.		

Chapter 17

Political Science

Local Politics

April 23

It was another lively City Council meeting. About midway through the meeting Mr. Williams shouted, "The Mayor is nothing more than a **figurehead**! We all know it's his wife who makes the decisions." The
5   Mayor jumped up and forcefully declared that Williams would never be able to **justify** such a ridiculous claim. Before pandemonium broke out, Councilmember Lopez calmed the mayor and the upset citizens. Luckily, her **charisma** usually keeps the more vocal citizens from disrupting the meetings. (And, dear editor, I'm not embellishing my notes.)

When the council returned
10   to the agenda, there was a long discussion on new construction, including height limits and locations. Mrs. Chen shared her opinion, hardly endorsed by others in the audience, that the council has a **bias** toward big business interests and that recent decisions are destroying the downtown's quaint appearance. Mr. Moore rose to say he also had misgivings about the council's abilities because not enough money is being devoted to the city's crumbling **infrastructure**. He listed a dozen roads, bridges, and facilities
15   that are in serious need of repair (possible article here). Just before the meeting adjourned, the always amiable Ms. Tate stood up saying she hoped to end the session on a positive note. She concisely explained that she has been "playing with the **notion** of a summer festival downtown." She suggested the festival include music, food and craft booths, and games for kids. Several citizens applauded, and Lopez agreed that this was an idea she would like to see the city implement.

May 21
20

This month's meeting started off with a surprising incident. Mr. Williams rose and loudly announced: "It is my duty as a citizen to **invoke** my First **Amendment*** right to free speech," and he did so by calling the mayor a "nincompoop." Despite his choice of names being outdated, it ignited the mayor's anger, and he yelled back, "Williams, you're the nincompoop!" Quick arms reached out to stop the
25   men from getting closer. As Williams was led out by friends, he shouted, "This city reached its **zenith** two years ago before Ed Miller was elected. It will go down in flames if he wins again!" After everyone settled down, the topic that consumed most of the meeting was the **impending** election (just two weeks away) and how voter apathy might endanger the tax proposal that would
30   increase funds for city parks and updated play equipment. The meeting ended quietly with a motion to move forward with plans for a summer festival.
(*Note to self: use a capital A when referring to one of the additions to the U.S. Constitution.)

Predicting

For each set, write the definition on the line next to the word to which it belongs. If you are unsure, return to the reading, and underline any context clues you find. After you've made your predictions, check your answers against the Word List at the end of the chapter. Place a checkmark in the box next to each word whose definition you missed. These are the words you'll want to study closely.

Set One

charm   foundations countries depend on   a preference   to show to be right or fair
a person in a position of leadership who has no real power

❑ 1. **figurehead** (line 4) _____

❑ 2. **justify** (line 6) _____

❑ 3. **charisma** (line 8) _____

❑ 4. **bias** (line 11) _____

❑ 5. **infrastructure** (line 14) _____

Set Two

the highest point   about to happen   an idea   to use for support
the formal alteration of a document

❑ 6. **notion** (line 17) _____

❑ 7. **invoke** (line 22) _____

❑ 8. **Amendment** (line 22) _____

❑ 9. **zenith** (line 27) _____

❑ 10. **impending** (line 29) _____

Self-Tests

> MyReadingLab Visit Chapter 17: Political Science in MyReadingLab to complete the Self-Test activities.

1 Put a T for true or F for false next to each sentence.

_____ 1. The Orpilla family has an impending vacation—the couple plan to travel to Europe when they retire in twenty years.

_____ 2. Most parents teach their children that even if a person calls the child a bad name, it doesn't justify hitting the person.

_____ 3. A person usually reaches the zenith of his or her career the second day on a job.

_____ 4. Acting on the notion to drop all of one's classes after getting a D on a test is a good idea.

_____ 5. It can be a wise choice to invoke one's right to a lawyer when facing a criminal charge.

_____ 6. Most notable leaders possess charisma (e.g., Franklin D. Roosevelt, Gandhi, Cleopatra).

_____ 7. The judge showed a bias by carefully listening to each side's case.

_____ 8. An amendment to a contract keeps the terms the same as the original document.

_____ 9. Being a figurehead would likely frustrate a person who wants to make changes in an organization.

_____ 10. A company's infrastructure can change dramatically when it is acquired by another company.

2 Match each vocabulary word with its synonym in Set One and its antonym in Set Two.

Synonyms

Set One

_____	1. charisma	a. defend
_____	2. infrastructure	b. allure
_____	3. invoke	c. impulse
_____	4. notion	d. call
_____	5. justify	e. foundation

Antonyms

Set Two

_____	6. impending	f. worsening
_____	7. figurehead	g. fairness
_____	8. bias	h. depths
_____	9. zenith	i. distant
_____	10. amendment	j. organizer

3 Fill in each blank with the appropriate vocabulary word. Use each word once.

VOCABULARY LIST

notion	infrastructure	charisma	invoked	zenith
bias	justify	figurehead	impending	Amendment

1. The Twenty-Second _____ to the U.S. Constitution limits the number of times a person can be elected president.

2. When I asked my husband to _____ his working such long hours, he said he was doing it to earn more money to take me on a special trip next year, but I want to spend more time with him now.

3. The members of the Coleman family have too many posts about _____ disasters in their lives. I'm going to find serenity by not reading their posts for awhile.

4. Anh's creative presentation had to _____ the judges because his cooking has never been good enough to win second place.

5. Bridges are an important part of a city's _____ mainly for transportation reasons, but some people also highly regard them for their visual appeal.

6. Despite the financial scandal, the mayor was elected to another term because of his
_____.

7. The artist _____ the aid of the muses as he stared at his blank canvas.

8. Although Gavin is a union representative, he is just a(n) _____ who has no real power to make changes.

9. The _____ that women were too delicate to take part in politics seems like such a silly idea now.

10. The actor felt he had reached the _____ of his career after he won an Academy Award.

Word Wise

Collocations

I am *bewildered by* Tatiana's actions. She is usually a smart woman, but lately she has been doing dumb things like forgetting to put gas in her car and replying to suspicious e-mails. (Chapter 16)

Several people joined the movement because of its *charismatic leader*, who inspired them to see that changes to the system are possible. (Chapter 17)

The city can fix our *crumbling infrastructure* if our taxes are used wisely. Our roads, pipes, and bridges have not been properly maintained for years. (Chapter 17)

Word Pairs

Zenith/Nadir: Zenith (Chapter 17) means "the highest point," while nadir means "the lowest point." Helen felt she had reached the zenith of her professional life when she was awarded a Nobel Prize. It was a far cry from the nadir when she was an alcoholic living on the streets.

Connotations and Denotations

Charisma (Chapter 17): denotation—"special quality of leadership that inspires devotion." Whom do you picture as a charismatic leader? People often see the word as applying to leaders such as John F. Kennedy, Nelson Mandela, and Eleanor Roosevelt (normally considered good people fighting for worthy causes). When someone is said to have charisma, it is generally considered a positive trait; however, the word can equally apply to Adolph Hitler, who is usually not highly regarded as a person. Yet Hitler had the ability to inspire the devotion of thousands of people, which fits the denotation of charisma.

Interesting Etymologies

Figurehead (Chapter 17) comes from the ornamental figureheads found on the front of sailing ships. These decorative figures (often of women's heads or upper bodies) did not serve any purpose in the operation of the ship, leading to the definition of figurehead as "a person in a position of leadership who has no real power."

Interactive Version: Imagine it is election time and local politics are heating up. Complete the sentence starters to reflect messages you might read on signs or in fliers, or hear on television or at rallies. Use at least one vocabulary word in each sentence, and try to use all ten words in total. Add word endings (i.e., -s, -ed) as needed.

EXAMPLE: The time is ripe for _a candidate who is more than a figurehead!_

1. Our city needs _____
2. It is time _____
3. Vote to _____
4. Our candidate _____
5. This election means _____
6. Join us _____
7. Your vote _____
8. Without new leadership _____
9. With change comes _____
10. Democracy means _____

Word Part Reminder

Below are a few exercises to help you review the word parts you have been learning. Fill in the missing word part from the list, and circle the meaning of the word part found in each sentence. Try to complete the questions without returning to the Word Parts chapter, but if you get stuck, look back at Chapter 14.

anti	don	voc	ia

1. The most _____al members at the City Council meetings don't hesitate to call other people names when they disagree with their ideas.

2. If Hiro is willing to give me a break and par_____ my bad mood last night, I promise I will be a better house guest.

3. The city isn't _____business, but we are against big companies coming in and pushing out local stores.

4. Luckily, my husband's condition isn't serious. He usually only experiences insomn_____ when he is really stressed at work.

Word List

amendment
[ə mend′ mənt]

n. 1. the formal alteration of a document; revision
2. the act of changing for the better; improvement

bias
[bī′ əs]

n. a preference or prejudice that can hinder impartial decision making; unfairness

v. to influence, usually in an unfair manner

charisma
[kə riz′ mə]

n. a special quality of leadership that inspires devotion; charm; allure

figurehead
[fig′ yər hed′]

n. a person in a position of leadership who has no real power

impending
[im pen′ding]

adj. 1. about to happen; approaching
2. threatening; looming

infrastructure
[in′ frə struk′ chər]

n. 1. foundations countries depend on, such as roads and power plants
2. the basic features of an organization

invoke
[in vōk′]

v. 1. to cite or use for support
2. to call on for support or inspiration; to summon

justify
[jus′ tə fī′]

v. to show or prove to be right or fair; to defend

notion
[nō′ shən]

n. 1. an idea, belief, or opinion
2. an impulse or urge

zenith
[zē′ nith]

n. the highest point; the peak; the top

Words to Watch

Which words would you like to practice with a bit more? Pick 3–5 words to study, and list them below. Write the word and its definition, and compose your own sentence using the word correctly. This extra practice could be the final touch to learning a word.

Word	Definition	Your Sentence
1.		
2.		
3.		
4.		
5.		

Chapter 18

Sports Medicine

Avoiding Injuries

Welcome! Now that you have signed up for the college's Get Fit program, it is time to begin training. Your greatest **asset**—enthusiasm—could become your biggest **liability** if you don't take a sensible approach to training. One problem to avoid is a sport's injury. If you have a
5   **propensity** to overdo it when starting something new, read these tips to avoid damaging your body.

EQUIPMENT: With training, people have the **capacity** to complete physical activities they never thought possible, but they need to invest in the proper equipment. Featured here are two key items. Stop by the
10   Athletic Center on campus for a full list of equipment suggestions.

Shoes: To prevent injuries make sure your shoes fit properly, have excellent arch support, and are designed for shock absorbency. Because the Get Fit program features many types of sports, consider buying a cross-training shoe. Check with the Athletic Center staff to make sure
15   your shoes are right for the sports you plan to try. If you ignore pain in your foot, knee, or back, your problems are likely to **proliferate** as these are key areas for sport's injuries.

Helmets: You need a helmet to participate in any of the program's bicycle events, including road and mountain bike rides. Head injuries are greatly reduced when people wear a helmet. Visit the Athletic Center for assistance on getting a helmet to fit properly.

20   **WEATHER:** When you **venture** outside for exercise, your body needs to adjust to the weather conditions.

Cold Days: Wear layers of clothing made of appropriate fabrics to prevent excessive heat lost. It is especially important to keep the head and hands warm, so wear a wool hat and gloves. Arrange to exercise with a friend since accidents can easily happen on slippery (wet or snowy) surfaces, making
25   it essential to have someone there to call for help. You may be tempted to train more in the winter to work off high-calorie treats, but give your body time to **recuperate** after hard workouts. Also get a good night's sleep to give the body and mind time to rest.

Hot Days: As the weather warms up, **acclimate** your body by gradually increasing the intensity of your workouts. It may take the body two weeks to adjust to higher temperatures. It is essential to
30   avoid dehydration by drinking enough fluids (water or sports drinks). Make sure to drink before, during, and after training or playing. Plan exercise times based on the temperature—get up early or wait until cooler evening temperatures on especially hot days. If you experience nausea, headaches, or dizziness, **cease** the activity and move to a cool or shady spot to rest.

      You have made a commitment to challenge yourself by joining the Get Fit program. The college
35   hopes that you will discover the physical and mental rewards of exercise by trying a variety of activities. Exercise produces chemicals that are pleasing to the brain (think of the runner's high). In order to preserve the **jovial** mood that comes from keeping fit, follow the above tips, and meet with a trainer if you experience any exercise-related pain.

Next week's topic: Nutrition Tips for Athletes

Predicting

For each set, write the definition on the line next to the word to which it belongs. If you are unsure, return to the reading, and underline any context clues you find. After you've made your predictions, check your answers against the Word List at the end of the chapter. Place a checkmark in the box next to each word whose definition you missed. These are the words you'll want to study closely.

Set One

a leaning	to grow	a desirable thing	the ability to do	a disadvantage

❑ 1. **asset** (line 2) _____

❑ 2. **liability** (line 3) _____

❑ 3. **propensity** (line 5) _____

❑ 4. **capacity** (line 7) _____

❑ 5. **proliferate** (line 16) _____

Set Two

to stop	to brave	cheerful	to adapt	to return to health

❑ 6. **venture** (line 20) _____

❑ 7. **recuperate** (line 26) _____

❑ 8. **acclimate** (line 28) _____

❑ 9. **cease** (line 33) _____

❑ 10. **jovial** (line 37) _____

Self-Tests

MyReadingLab Visit Chapter 18: Sports Medicine in MyReadingLab to complete the Self-Test activities.

1 Circle the correct meaning of each vocabulary word.

1. asset: a worthless thing   a desirable thing

2. jovial: good-humored   sad

3. acclimate: reject   adjust

4. proliferate: to decrease   to increase

5. propensity: a preference   an aversion

6. venture: to fear   to brave

7. capacity: ability   inability

8. recuperate: worsen   recover

9. liability: a disadvantage   an advantage

10. cease: discontinue   begin

2 Finish the readings using the vocabulary words. Use each word once.

Set One

VOCABULARY LIST

jovial	asset	venture	capacity	acclimate

I'm glad we arrived a few days before the tour started to help us (1)_____ to the high-altitude air. I have been breathing a little harder than usual, but it certainly would have been worse if we had just arrived. All the training we did at home has certainly been a big (2)_____. In a few days I should be able to keep up with the best riders in the group, at least for a few miles.

However, this is such a(n) (3)_____ group of people that I could ride alongside any of them and have a good time. We were lucky that the company let the two of us in even though the trip was filled to (4)_____. At one time I was really nervous about being able to ride thirty-plus miles every day for two weeks, but now I know we did the right thing by embarking on this (5)_____. It won't be our last bicycle trip.

Set Two

VOCABULARY LIST

cease	liability	recuperate	propensity	proliferate

I injured my knee playing soccer and had to have an operation. Now the doctor says I have to give my body at least six month to fully (6)_____. He said I should (7)_____ any activities that put pressure on my knee. I had hoped to stay in shape by playing soccer, but my attempt to stay healthy has become a (8)_____. The doctor did recommend yoga with easy stretches. I joined a class, but on the third session I fell over while doing the tree pose and bruised my elbow and hip. Now I feel like I have a (9)_____ for injuries. Maybe my injuries won't (10)_____ if I stick to chess or checkers as my newest "sports."

3 For each set, complete the analogies. See Completing Analogies on page 6 for instructions and practice.

Set One

1. a flat tire : arrive late :: faulty part : _____ production
2. a raise : benefit :: a broken leg : _____
3. cancel : erase :: capability : _____
4. ASAP : acronym :: a sea voyage : _____
5. forget a birthday : apologize :: move to a new country: _____

VOCABULARY LIST

capacity	cease
liability	acclimate
venture	

Set Two

6. spinach : vegetable :: a college degree : _____

7. athlete : train :: gambler : _____ losses

8. in a traffic jam : angry :: at a party : _____

9. pardon : forgive :: tendency : _____

10. humble : proud :: _____ : decline

VOCABULARY LIST

jovial   asset

proliferate   recuperate

propensity

Word Visions

Identify the two vocabulary words represented in the drawings.

1. _____

2. _____

Word Wise

Collocations

After her business partner left town, Tammy knew it was time to *venture out* on her own, but she was still nervous about what she would encounter. (Chapter 18)

We should have anticipated that the auditorium would be *filled to capacity* since the program features three major athletes as well as leading coaches and sports medicine doctors. (Chapter 18)

I thought all my problems would *cease to exist* once I moved, and though some are gone, I found a few news ones. (Chapter 18)

Word Pairs

Asset/Liability: Asset (Chapter 18) means "a desirable thing or quality," and liability (Chapter 18) means "a disadvantage; an undesirable thing." Reynaldo's greatest asset is his friendliness; he can charm anyone. His greatest liability is his stubbornness; he won't change his mind even when he knows he is wrong.

Interesting Etymologies

Jovial (Chapter 18) comes from the Latin *Jovialis,* "of Jupiter." Jupiter was the Roman god of the sky. According to astrological beliefs, those born under the sign of Jupiter were supposed to be happy people, so jovial came to mean "merry; good-humored."

Interactive Exercise

The college sent out a follow-up questionnaire about student experiences during the Get Fit program. Imagine that you joined the program to help you answer the questions. Use at least seven of the vocabulary words in your responses.

1. What was your greatest asset for participating in the various sports and activities? What was your greatest liability?

   _____

   _____

2. What are two methods you used to recuperate after a hard workout?

   _____

   _____

3. What did you do to acclimate to the weather changes as the program moved from winter to spring?

   _____

4. Did any health problems cease to exist once you began participating in the program? Was there a proliferation of any health problems during the program?

   _____

   _____

5. What sport had the most jovial participants? What do you think made them so merry?

   _____

   _____

6. Participating in which of the following activities caused or would cause you to venture out of your comfort zone: downhill skiing, football, golfing, soccer, horseback riding? Briefly explain why.

   _____

   _____

7. Do you feel that participating in the Get Fit program increased your propensity to exercise? What makes you feel this way?

   _____

   _____

8. Next year the college is considering the addition of a10K run to celebrate the end of the program. In what capacity would you be willing to participate in the run (consider areas from organizing, to staffing, or entering the race)?

   _____

   _____

Conversation Starters

An excellent way to review the vocabulary words and help to make them your own is to use them when you are speaking. Gather three to five friends or classmates, and use one or more of the conversation starters below. Before you begin talking, have each person write down six of the vocabulary words he or she will use during the conversation. Share your lists with each other to check that you did not all pick the same six words. Try to cover all of the words you want to study, whether you are reviewing one, two, or more chapters.

1. How does your writing differ from the language you use when speaking? Do colloquialisms and clichés play a role in these differences?
2. What are a few current political issues in your area? Which issue deserves the most attention?
3. What are three sports or other types of exercise that you enjoy? What makes these activities fun?

Word List

acclimate
[ak′ lə māt′, ə klī′ mit]
v. to get used to a new setting or situation; to adapt; to adjust

asset
[as′ et]
n. an advantage; a desirable thing or quality

capacity
[kə pas′ i tē]
n. 1. the ability to do or make something; capability
2. the ability to hold something
3. the position in which a person functions; role

cease
[sēs]
v. to put an end to; to stop; to discontinue

jovial
[jō′ vē əl]
adj. merry; good-humored; cheerful

liability
[lī′ ə bil′ i tē]
n. a disadvantage; an undesirable thing or quality

proliferate
[prə lif′ ə rāt′]
v. to increase in number; to spread rapidly; to grow

propensity
[prə pen′ si tē]
n. a tendency; a leaning; a preference

recuperate
[ri kōō′ pə rāt′, -kyōō′-]
v. 1. to return to health or regain strength; to recover
2. to recover from a financial loss

venture
[ven′ chər]
v. to brave; to take the risk of
n. an undertaking involving risk; a business project

Words to Watch

Which words would you like to practice with a bit more? Pick 3–5 words to study, and list them below. Write the word and its definition, and compose your own sentence using the word correctly. This extra practice could be the final touch to learning a word.

Word	Definition	Your Sentence
1. _____	_____	_____
2. _____	_____	_____
3. _____	_____	_____
4. _____	_____	_____
5. _____	_____	_____

Chapter 19

Review

Focus on Chapters 16–18

The following activities give you the opportunity to further interact with the vocabulary words you've been learning. By taking tests, answering questions, using visuals, doing a crossword puzzle, and working with others, you will see which words you know well and which ones need additional study.

Self-Tests MyReadingLab Visit Chapter 19: Review in MyReadingLab to complete the Self-Test activities.

LO 4,8 1 Match each term with its synonym in Set One and its antonym in Set Two.

Synonyms

Set One

_____ 1. scrutinize a. summary

_____ 2. charisma b. inspect

_____ 3. justify c. charm

_____ 4. synopsis d. leaning

_____ 5. propensity e. defend

Antonyms

Set Two

_____ 6. jovial f. explain

_____ 7. bewilder g. lengthy

_____ 8. bias h. weaken

_____ 9. concise i. sad

_____ 10. recuperate j. fairness

Remember to add words to Word Reactions on page 175 after completing the Review chapter activities.

LO 1 **2** Pick the word that best completes each sentence.

1. It can take some students two or three semesters to _____ to a college environment.

   a. cease   b. acclimate   c. bewilder   d. invoke

2. I appreciated the _____ when my friend said, "I'm going to have fun at the dentist today!" I knew, like me, that he wouldn't really get any enjoyment out of the visit.

   a. bias   b. irony   c. propensity   d. charisma

3. Will's _____ to take off on a road trip had people wondering why he didn't make it to the graduation ceremony.

   a. homonym   b. propensity   c. zenith   d. notion

4. Some people say I am a _____ to the team, but I don't think it is a disadvantage to have me on the team, despite my failure to make four easy goals and then making one for the other team.

   a. liability   b. cliché   c. bias   d. figurehead

5. After the _____ was made to the motion, representatives on both sides voted for its passage.

   a. venture   b. propensity   c. amendment   d. euphemism

6. I hated to see the _____ DNF next to my name at the end of the race, but my left knee began to hurt so much I just could not finish.

   a. acronym   b. capacity   c. notion   d. asset

7. Bridges are an important part of the _____ for cities that are located near rivers or large lakes.

   a. liability   b. irony   c. infrastructure   d. figurehead

8. I try to avoid using _____ in my college papers, but occasionally a word like "gonna" slips in.

   a. amendments   b. homonyms   c. figureheads   d. colloquialisms

LO 1 **3** Pick the vocabulary word that best completes the sentence. Use each word once.

propensity	figurehead	asset	capacity	homonym

1. Alejandro had been a major _____ to this project thanks to his concise observations.

2. The _____ pair that gives me the most trouble is *hear* and *here*.

3. I know you have the _____ to learn the material; you just need to apply yourself.

4. There is a(n) _____ among students to put off writing a paper until the day before it is due.

5. As president, Victor was only a(n) _____; the person with the real power was his brother, who held the title of vice president.

LO 4 **4** Complete the following sentences that illustrate collocations. The rest of the collocation is in italics. Use each word once.

bewildered	charismatic	venture	infrastructure	capacity	cease

1. When I looked out and saw that the room was *filled to* _____, I became even more nervous about performing.

2. I was afraid to _____ *out* on my own when I first went to school in Madrid, but as my Spanish got better, I felt more confident about visiting places alone.

3. Martin Luther King Jr. was a _____ *leader* who encouraged people to rally in support of civil rights.

4. I was _____ *by* Sid's actions. He is usually such a calm man, but lately he has been acting extremely nervous.

5. If humans don't work to save endangered animals, many types could _____ *to exist* within a few years.

6. If we don't do something about the *crumbling* _____ in this state, we can expect to see several accidents due to bridges and roads collapsing.

LO 5 **5** Fill in the missing word part, and circle the meaning of the word part found in each sentence. Use one of the word parts twice.

vent	fer	pend	cis	vok	ism	pens

1. Lee in_____ed a rarely used clause in the company manual which states that meetings will not take place on Friday afternoons unless the matter is urgent. He then called for an end to the meeting and to all others that were scheduled for the rest of the month.

2. I only had time to give a con_____e report on what happened at the morning meeting. I had to cut my report short because of an emergency in the marketing department.

3. The number of visitors continues to proli_____ate each month. Our campaign to bring more people to town by having varied weekend festivals has really worked.

4. My latest _____ure, a donut cart at the Saturday farmer's market, will help me to move toward opening two more bakeries in the area by getting my name before the public.

5. My im_____ing visit to the dentist has been weighing on my mind. I haven't been in three years, and I am afraid the dentist is going to discover a cavity.

6. When my friend moved here from the South, he often used the colloquial_____ "y'all," but this practice has diminished quite a bit during the six years he has lived in Vermont.

7. Zita's pro_____ity to hang out at dance clubs nearly every night until two or three in the morning is hurting her school work.

8. When a person uses a euphem_____, the action may help him or her cope with a difficult situation, such as death or an illness.

6 Finish the story using the vocabulary words below. Use each word once.

VOCABULARY LIST

irony	impending	notion	acronym	assets
scrutinize	liability	cease	zenith	cliché

Beyond the Garden Gate

I awoke, as the (1)_____ goes,

feeling as fresh as a daisy. Then I remembered the

(2)_____ garden tour. It was only a few

days away. I wondered what had given me the crazy

(3)_____ to let GAB into my yard. Really

GAB is the perfect (4)_____ for the

Garden Around Back club. Most of the members do more

talking than gardening. I was sure they were going to

(5)_____ every inch of my garden and

find fault with my flowers, gazebo, and waterfall.

I have several pieces of garden art that I made out of

trowels, hoses, rakes, and other tools. I consider them

(6)_____ that make my garden special.

Now I was wondering if others would see them as a(n)

(7)_____. I was so worried about people's reactions

to my garden that the day before the event I almost called to cancel,

but I had promised to be part of the tour, and it was too late to

back out.

The big day arrived, and the weather was wonderful. The

flowers looked spectacular. I decided that the sensible move was

to (8)_____ worrying and enjoy the beauty of my

garden. People started arriving early in the morning and continued

streaming through all day. And the great (9)_____ is

that everyone was so friendly and complimentary about every part

of the garden. Several people told me they wished they could grow lilies like mine. Instead of

being the dreadful day I had imagined, it might well be the (10)_____ of my time

as a gardener.

Interactive Exercise

LO 2 Answer the following questions to further test your understanding of the vocabulary words.

1. What are two areas where people tend to have a strong bias?

   _____

   _____

2. What type of situation would justify missing a deadline at work or school?

   _____

   _____

3. Which cliché do you often find yourself using? Why do you think that is?

   _____

   _____

4. Under what conditions do you think a company would hire someone as a figurehead instead of letting the person have real control?

   _____

   _____

5. Name three people you consider charismatic leaders from any time period.

   _____

   _____

6. What are two reasons a person's problems might proliferate?

   _____

   _____

7. What are two items you would take to a friend who is in the hospital recuperating from an operation?

   _____

   _____

8. List two euphemisms you have used or encountered.

   _____

   _____

9. If you could propose an amendment to the Constitution what would it be? Why is this change necessary?

   _____

   _____

10. Give a synopsis of a book or story you have enjoyed reading.

   _____

   _____

   _____

LO 6 **Associations**

Use four words from the list below to write four
sentences that compare or contrast the two photographs.
Write the words you want to use on the middle lines. This exercise calls on your critical- and
creative-thinking skills to make associations between the photos and words.

EXAMPLES: The cliché "because it's there" is used to explain why people climb mountains, and it
can also apply to why people eat large amounts of food. (Comparison)

A person would need to acclimate in order to climb a mountain, but for most people no
adjustment is needed to enjoy a big sandwich. (Contrast)

_____

_____

_____

_____

VOCABULARY LIST

euphemism	homonym	scrutinize	cliché	colloquialism
notion	infrastructure	cease	zenith	acclimate
asset	jovial	liability	proliferate	invoke

Your sentences:

_____

_____

_____

_____

_____

_____

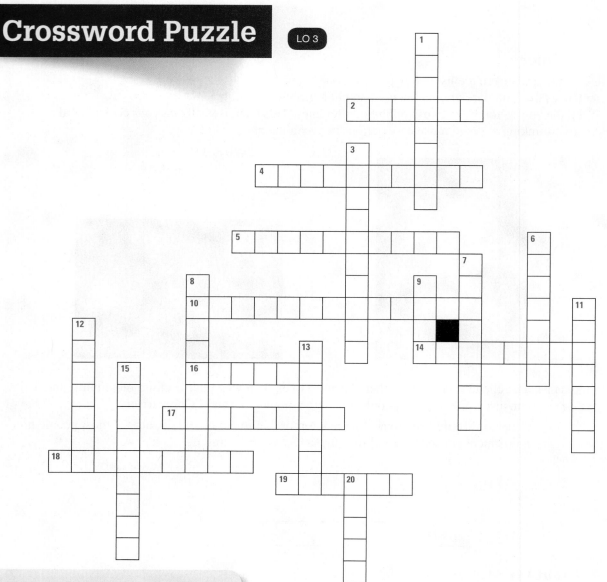

Use the following words to complete the crossword puzzle. Use each word once.

VOCABULARY LIST

acclimate	impending
acronym	invoke
amendment	irony
bias	jovial
bewilder	justify
capacity	propensity
colloquialism	recuperate
concise	synopsis
figurehead	venture
homonyms	zenith

Across

2. merry and cheerful
4. a person in a position of leadership who has no real power
5. what a patient or business owner with slow sales needs
10. "There ain't nothin' to see here."
14. a summary
16. to use or call on for support
17. "I'm the head of the accounting department."
18. can add this to a document
19. the highest point

Down

1. to confuse or puzzle
3. a tendency
6. opposite of wordy
7. to, too, two
8. to the weather or a new job, as examples
9. "Let's buy the house with the red door because I love red!"
11. to show or prove to be right or fair
12. RSVP or NBA, as examples
13. an undertaking involving risk
15. opposite of distant
20. a clash between expectation and reality

HINT

Mistakes Are Learning Experiences

Making mistakes is part of the learning process. When you learned to ride a bike, you probably fell over a few times before you learned to keep your balance. The same idea applies to learning vocabulary. When you take a test, you may not get a perfect score. Look at the mistakes you made. Try to decide what went wrong. Did you read a question too fast? Did you misunderstand a question? Did you not study enough? Don't be so disappointed in a bad grade that you can't learn from the experience. You will do better next time if you take the time to understand what you did wrong this time. Also ask your instructor if you are unsure about why you got a question wrong; he or she wants to help you do better next time.

Mix It Up   LO 2,3,7

Motivating with Music

If you enjoy music, select some of your favorite tunes and get together with four or five classmates to see how music can aid in learning. Besides the music, you will need something to play it on, paper, and pens.

Decide on which words you want to study. If you are reviewing several chapters, each person should pick different vocabulary words to use so the group can cover more of the words. While the music plays, write a story that the music inspires using six or seven of the words to be studied (you may choose to write six or seven sentences each using a vocabulary word instead of writing a story). The ideas for the story or sentences may come from the tone of the music or the thoughts expressed in a song's lyrics. Read your stories or sentences to each other, and discuss the ideas the music brought out in relation to the vocabulary words. It is interesting to hear the similarities and differences the music inspires within the group. To review more words, pick another piece of music and do the activity again.

Classical music works well, but music related to a chapter may also serve as inspiration and possibly as a memory aid. For example, use contemporary music containing wordplay for relating to Chapter 16, patriotic music for Chapter 17, and songs played in stadiums (e.g., Queen's "We Are the Champions"), or tunes that motivate you to exercise for Chapter 18. Have fun exploring how music, writing, and learning vocabulary can be creatively combined.

Chapter 20

Nutrition

Healthy Eating

A healthy diet isn't that hard to achieve, and it has many rewards. Eating the right foods can ward off problems such as heart disease, bone loss, and various kinds of cancers. It can also prevent shortages in necessary miner-
5 als. For example, an iron **deficiency** can result in **anemia**, a common condition that leaves a person feeling continually tired. For **optimum** health, eat a diverse diet to get all of the vitamins and minerals your body needs to perform its best. Below are the types of foods you want to eat
10 regularly and suggestions of ways to easily integrate these foods into your daily meals.

Fruits and Vegetables: The best **antidote** for a variety of health concerns is to put fruits and vegetables on the top of your to-eat list. Fruits and vegetables provide numerous nutrients, including vitamin A to make skin and eyes healthy and vitamin C to support teeth
15 and gums. A **comprehensive** meal plan will include fruits and vegetables in a variety of colors—green, yellow, orange, red, blue, and purple—to provide a range of minerals and vitamins. To encourage daily snacking, keep an **eclectic** supply of fruits on hand, such as kiwis, bananas, mangoes, apricots, cherries, blueberries, plums, and prunes. For vegetables consider these choices for color variety: broccoli, carrots, red bell peppers, and eggplant. Eat your fruits and vegetables raw or lightly steamed to maintain their
20 high nutritional value. **Throughout the Day:** blueberries on breakfast cereal, roasted sweet potato fries for lunch, red bell peppers piled on green leaf lettuce at dinner, and an orange for a snack.

Whole Grains: The benefits of whole grains include carbohydrates that provide the body with energy and B vitamins that strengthen the nervous system. Whole grains include whole wheat bread, brown rice, popcorn, quinoa, and oatmeal. Whole grains have more nutrients, such as fiber and vitamin E,
25 than their white counterparts. **Throughout the Day:** oatmeal for breakfast, brown rice to **complement** a plate of steamed vegetables at lunch, whole wheat pasta for dinner, and popcorn as a snack.

Dairy Products: Don't limit the **domain** of your dairy products to the breakfast table. Dairy prod-ucts supply calcium to build strong bones, and low-fat versions can help to fight high blood pressure. Dairy products include milk, yogurt, and cheese. Soy drinks can also supply calcium and vitamin
30 D; check the Nutritional Facts label to see if the soy product has been fortified with these nutrients.
Throughout the Day: skim or soy milk in a smoothie for breakfast, Swiss cheese on whole wheat bread for lunch, cottage cheese with tomato slices as a dinner side, and low-fat yogurt with fresh peaches for a snack.

Finally, with a **finite** number of calories available in a
35 sensible diet, you want to make smart choices. Read nutri-tional labels to learn portion sizes, calories, fat grams, and salt content. What looks like a single serving may surpris-ingly be labeled as three servings. In general, eat more naturally by choosing foods with the least processing.
40 Healthy eating will increase your **longevity** and make your later years happy ones.

Predicting

For each set, write the definition on the line next to the word to which it belongs. If you are unsure, return to the reading, and underline any context clues you find. After you've made your predictions, check your answers against the Word List at the end of the chapter. Place a checkmark in the box next to each word whose definition you missed. These are the words you'll want to study closely.

Set One

complete	most favorable	a cure
shortage	a lack of oxygen-carrying material in the blood, which results in weakness	

- ❑ 1. **deficiency** (line 5) _____
- ❑ 2. **anemia** (line 5) _____
- ❑ 3. **optimum** (line 7) _____
- ❑ 4. **antidote** (line 12) _____
- ❑ 5. **comprehensive** (line 15) _____

Set Two

length of life	diverse	limited	territory of control	to balance or complete

- ❑ 6. **eclectic** (line 17) _____
- ❑ 7. **complement** (line 25) _____
- ❑ 8. **domain** (line 27) _____
- ❑ 9. **finite** (line 34) _____
- ❑ 10. **longevity** (line 40) _____

Self-Tests

> **MyReadingLab** Visit Chapter 20: Nutrition in MyReadingLab to complete the Self-Test activities.

1 Write the letter of the vocabulary word next to the situation that relates to it. Use each word once.

Set One

_____	1. The test will cover material from the entire term.	a. eclectic
_____	2. The resort offers diverse activities, from chess to volleyball.	b. deficiency
_____	3. In order to live to one hundred, I'm eating right and exercising daily.	c. longevity
_____	4. The doctor said I'm low in the B vitamins and iron.	d. comprehensive
_____	5. A weekly massage proved to be the cure for Cam's stress.	e. antidote

Set Two

_____ 6. Mary Ann looks pale, and she has no energy or strength.   f. optimum

_____ 7. Rice goes well with fish dishes.   g. domain

_____ 8. There is only so much room in a box.   h. finite

_____ 9. Since I'm always home at 8 a.m. that is the best time to call.   i. anemia

_____ 10. The grill is my husband's territory; it is where he is king.   j. complement

2 Fill in each blank with the appropriate vocabulary word. Use each word once.

VOCABULARY LIST

domain	anemia	complement	eclectic	finite
optimum	deficiency	longevity	comprehensive	antidote

As a reliable (1)_____ to
a depressing gray day, I decided to have
a party. I called my friends and asked
everyone to bring a dish to share.
I was sure we would end up with a(n)
(2)_____ menu. Because Meg
is suffering from (3)_____,
I decided to provide some iron-rich foods,
like clams, lentils, and a strawberry and
spinach salad. I also made my favorite
mushroom side dish since it serves as the perfect (4)_____ to almost any food. Once
the guests began arriving and placing their dishes on the table, I knew that there wouldn't be a(n)
(5)_____ of delicious and nutritious food.

      After dinner we decided to share dreams about our retirement years. Since we all eat right
and exercise regularly, we knew (6)_____ was something we should count on. There
are, however, only a(n) (7)_____ number of years for all of us, so we should plan
for the things we really want to do. Jo said that in her sixties and beyond she saw the water as her
(8)_____. She was looking forward to teaching kids how to swim and competing in
swimming events at the Senior Olympics. Chen revealed that he would be looking for a(n)
(9)_____ performance car because he planned to drive from Alaska to the tip of South
America and have several adventures along the way. I explained that I was already at work on a(n)
(10)_____ plan that would allow me to travel for months at a time and eventually let me
visit every country in the world.

3 Finish the following analogies. See Completing Analogies on page 6 for instructions. Use each word once.

VOCABULARY LIST

finite	longevity	antidote	deficiency	comprehensive
anemia	eclectic	domain	complement	optimum

1. huge : immense :: diverse : _____
2. a power failure : dead phone lines :: eating healthy : _____
3. disappointed : pleased :: _____ : abundance
4. shovel : dig :: _____ : save a life
5. polka : dance :: Web site address : _____
6. poor : rich :: partial : _____
7. pineapple : fruit :: space in a closet : _____
8. mouse : small animal :: sunshine for an outdoor wedding : _____ condition
9. lack of studying : bad grades :: _____ : weakness
10. compliment : praise :: _____ : balance

Word Wise

Context Clue Mini-Lesson 5

This lesson combines the techniques you have practiced in the four previous lessons. You will be looking for synonyms, antonyms, general meaning, and examples (SAGE) to help you understand the underlined words. In the paragraph below, circle any clues you find and then write the types of clues and your definitions on the lines next to the words that follow the paragraph.

The company can no longer tolerate your recent <u>unscrupulous</u> behavior. We have discovered that you have been stealing company supplies, taking three-hour lunches, and viewing inappropriate material on the Internet on company time. Because of your long association with the firm, we are giving you the opportunity to leave of your own <u>volition</u>. If you do not resign by Tuesday, you will be fired by the end of the week. We do not want to create unnecessary <u>acrimony</u> between you and the company. To maintain some harmony in our relationship, we will be having a small going-away party for you on Thursday. I'm sorry these last few months have had to <u>mar</u> an otherwise positive working relationship, but the damage has been done, and it is time for you to leave.

Type of Context Clue and Your Definition

1. Unscrupulous _____
2. Volition _____
3. Acrimony _____
4. Mar _____

Interactive Version: Use some of the foods in the photograph to write two entries in a food journal. Elements you can consider writing about include what you ate, when you ate, how nutritious the foods were, and their impact on your health. Use at least six of the vocabulary words in your entries.

Entry 1: _____

_____

_____

_____

_____

Entry 2: _____

_____

_____

_____

_____

HINT

Study Groups

A class can be more rewarding if you find classmates to study with. To create effective study groups, keep these points in mind.

- Have those who are interested in forming a group list their best times to meet. Pick a time that can accommodate most people; it may be impossible to get everyone together all the time.
- Decide how often you will meet—twice a week, once a week, once a month. Exchange phone numbers and e-mail addresses to announce meeting times.
- Pick a place that promotes studying. See whether the library has study group rooms. Find a place where you won't be interrupted by friends, children, or other distractions.
- Bring the necessary books, notes, and other materials to each session.
- Assign someone to monitor the time and to remind people to keep conversations on topic. Ask anyone to leave who does not really want to study.
- Evaluate how useful each study session is and decide what changes may be needed for the next time.

Word List

anemia
[ə nē′ mē ə]
n. a lack of oxygen-carrying material in the blood, which results in weakness

antidote
[an′ ti dōt′]
n. 1. something that prevents an unwanted effect; a cure
2. a medicine or other remedy for counteracting the effects of a poison or a disease

complement
[kom′ plə mənt]
v. to serve as a completion to; to balance or complete
n. something that completes or makes up a whole

comprehensive
[kom′ pri hen′ siv]
adj. large in content or reach; complete; full

deficiency
[di fish′ ən sē]
n. a lack or shortage

domain
[dō mān′]
n. 1. a territory of control; a kingdom
2. an area of concern; a field

eclectic
[i klek′ tik]
adj. selecting from various sources; diverse

finite
[fī′ nīt′]
adj. 1. having boundaries; limited
2. existing for a limited time; temporary

longevity
[lon jev′ i tē, lôn-]
n. long life; length of life or service

optimum
[op′ tə məm]
adj. most favorable; best
n. the best condition or amount for a specific situation

Words to Watch

Which words would you like to practice with a bit more? Pick 3–5 words to study, and list them below. Write the word and its definition, and compose your own sentence using the word correctly. This extra practice could be the final touch to learning a word.

Word	Definition	Your Sentence
1. _____	_____	_____
_____		_____
2. _____	_____	_____
_____		_____
3. _____	_____	_____
_____		_____
4. _____	_____	_____
_____		_____
5. _____	_____	_____
_____		_____

Chapter 21

City Planning

Public Input

Upcoming Design Meeting

We invite the public's input on a proposal for the renewal of the 22nd block of Evergreen Avenue. The plan calls for condominiums, office space, and retail shops. The goal is to bring people back to the **urban** center and create a community where people can live, work, shop, and play. For several years, people have been moving out of the downtown core for the suburbs. With increases in traffic congestion and higher gas prices, many people are no longer willing to **endure** long commutes and the hassles associated with living outside of the city. To **rectify** this problem, we are creating a place where people will want to live.

1. We conducted several surveys to get a **consensus** on the services people desire in downtown living. People agreed that they want places to relax. The twelve-story residential building will feature a rooftop garden with **panoramic** views of the bay and surrounding mountains and plenty of chairs to take in the views. There will also be a space for residents to tend small garden plots to grow fresh fruits and vegetables. The entire complex will have green areas where people can relax in the shade of a tree or enjoy the serenity found in listening to a fountain.

2. People desire a sense of community. The **edifice** we are proposing will include a central room where residents can chat, play pool or ping pong, and watch movies on a large-screen television. Glass and steal will be combined for an open feel for the entire complex. The building will exemplify the best in green technology and energy-efficient systems. We consider our design the **definitive** response to the needs of people and the environment.

3. People want activities close by. Evergreen Plaza will be a **gateway** to downtown attractions. From here residents can easily walk or use public transportation to visit downtown sights, including the art museum, ballpark, and science center. Several movie and live theaters are within a three-block walk. A mixed-use building on the site will provide a grocery, coffee bar, restaurants, and specialty stores. As the city continues to **revitalize** downtown, Evergreen Plaza will play a prominent role in the process.

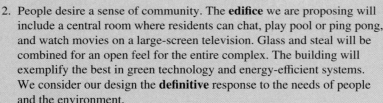

The meeting will **convene** May 23, at 6 p.m. at City Hall. The first hour will feature a synopsis of the plans, including sketches of the proposed buildings and photographs of the plants and fountains that will be installed. We will elicit questions from the public starting at seven. We eagerly await your advice as phase two of this exciting project begins.

Predicting

For each set, write the definition on the line next to the word to which it belongs. If you are unsure, return to the reading, and underline any context clues you find. After you've made your predictions, check your answers against the Word List at the end of the chapter. Place a checkmark in the box next to each word whose definition you missed. These are the words you'll want to study closely.

Set One

extensive	to correct	agreement	to tolerate	concerned with a city

☐ 1. **urban** (line 2) _____

☐ 2. **endure** (line 5) _____

☐ 3. **rectify** (line 6) _____

☐ 4. **consensus** (line 7) _____

☐ 5. **panoramic** (line 10) _____

Set Two

most reliable or complete	to renew	a building	a way to enter or gain access	to assemble

☐ 6. **edifice** (line 15) _____

☐ 7. **definitive** (line 20) _____

☐ 8. **gateway** (line 22) _____

☐ 9. **revitalize** (line 28) _____

☐ 10. **convene** (line 30) _____

Self-Tests

MyReadingLab Visit Chapter 21: City Planning in MyReadingLab to complete the Self-Test activities.

1 Find the synonym or definition in each sentence and replace it by writing the corresponding vocabulary word on the blank line. Use each word once.

VOCABULARY LIST

endure	revitalize	panoramic	consensus	urban
definitive	gateway	edifice	convene	rectify

1. City life is fun, but sometimes it is nice to get out in the countryside. _____

2. The salesman had to suffer several doors slammed in his face before he made his first sale. _____

3. The view from the top of the mountain was scenic. _____

4. I wasn't sure how to fix the problem, so I talked to my boss about possible solutions. _____

5. The concert hall is the largest and grandest structure in town. _____

VOCABULARY LIST

endure	revitalize	panoramic	consensus	urban
definitive	gateway	edifice	convene	rectify

6. Everyone is going to meet at my house, and then we will carpool to the play. _____

7. When I want the most reliable information on how to fix my car, I go to my dad. He has been working on cars for forty years. _____

8. We were able to reach an agreement on what to get grandma for her 80th birthday after an hour of discussing possible gifts. _____

9. When I heard that the town of Worthington was going to invigorate its downtown, I didn't expect it to look like a Swiss village. _____

10. My opening came when a new manager was hired who wanted people on the design team with bold ideas, like the ones I have. _____

Word Visions

Identify the two vocabulary words represented in the photographs.

1. _____

2. _____

2 Finish the sentences about some of the world's most amazing edifices. Use each word once.

VOCABULARY LIST

convene	revitalized	panoramic	consensus	edifice
definitive	gateway	endure	urban	rectify

1. Efforts to _____ problems with portions of the Great Wall in China have run into problems due to official procedures.

2. The Empire State building has been a part of New York City's _____ skyline since the 1930s.

3. After initial mixed reviews, Australians have reached a _____ that the Sydney Opera House is a building to be proud of.

4. Suggestions that parts of Machu Picchu be _____ to show what it looked like at the time of the Incas have been firmly turned down.

5. The Arch in St. Louis is a _____ to the West.

6. The Eiffel Tower offers _____ views of Paris.

7. There is still no _____ answer on how the pyramids in Egypt were built.

8. Opened in 1888 and designed to look like a Scottish castle, Canada's Banff Springs Hotel is an impressive _____ nestled in the Rocky Mountains.

9. Visitors often have to _____ heat and long lines to tour the Taj Mahal in India, but the magnificence of the building makes the hardships worth it.

10. On New Year's Eve, people in Seattle _____ at the foot of the Space Needle to watch fireworks shoot from the top of it.

3 For each set, write the letter of the most logical analogy. See Completing Analogies on page 6 for instructions.

Set One

1. last : endure ::	_____	a. dictionary : to find definitive spellings
2. arch : gateway ::	_____	b. disagreement : consensus
3. spatula : to turn a pancake ::	_____	c. ball : toy
4. neglected buildings : revitalize ::	_____	d. feeling ill : visit a doctor
5. dark : light ::	_____	e. combination : mixture

Set Two

6. musician : performs ::	_____	f. a street : busy
7. pants : clothing ::	_____	g. mansion : edifice
8. quit : stop ::	_____	h. lovely : ugly
9. worsen : rectify ::	_____	i. meeting : convenes
10. a meadow : panoramic ::	_____	j. city : urban

Word Wise

Collocations

The school district is working on a *comprehensive plan* to integrate writing assignments into every course, including physical education. (Chapter 20)

There is a definite *deficiency in* math skills among the latest graduating class; only 33% passed the state exam. (Chapter 20)

After three hours of discussion, the committee *reached a consensus* on whom to invite as the main speaker for the conference. (Chapter 21)

The story of the alligator that crawls out of the sewer and eats a baby is an *urban legend*. (Chapter 21)

Interactive Exercise

Answer the following questions as if you are the city planner. You can use the city you live in to develop your answers or create a fictitious city. Use at least two of the vocabulary words in each response.

1. What is the biggest problem in your urban area? What can you do to rectify it?

   _____

   _____

   _____

2. What kind of new edifice does your city need most? Why? Do you think there would be a consensus among the citizens about your decision?

   _____

   _____

   _____

3. What kind of problems might you have to endure as you revitalize the downtown area?

   _____

   _____

4. Do you need to design a building, plaza, or park to give people a better place to convene? What could it have a panoramic view of?

   _____

   _____

5. What kind of building, sculpture, or monument would best serve as a gateway to the downtown? Why would your idea be considered the definitive choice?

   _____

   _____

   _____

Word Part Reminder

Below are a few exercises to help you review the word parts you have been learning. Fill in the missing word part from the list, and circle the meaning of the word part found in each sentence. This reminder focuses on roots from all three Word Parts chapters. Try to complete the questions without returning to a Word Parts chapter; however, if you need help refer to the Word Parts list on page 178 to find the page numbers for the word parts.

| vent | vert | cred | fin |

1. It was a good thing I decided to turn my coffee cup over. If I had not in_____ed it, I might have been tempted to drink more than I should have the next time the waiter came by with the pot.

2. I could no longer believe Jenny when she told me the in_____ible story that she was late because she had been captured by aliens.

3. I decided to limit myself to one piece of candy a day. For the first week, I found it really hard to con_____e myself to such a small amount.

4. So far we know that 300 people are going to come to the con_____ion this summer.

Word List

consensus
[kən sen′ səs]
n. a unity of opinion; agreement; harmony

convene
[kən vēn′]
v. 1. to assemble, usually for a public purpose; to organize
2. to summon to appear

definitive
[di fin′ ə tiv]
adj. most reliable or complete; final

edifice
[e′ də fis]
n. a building or a structure, usually used when referring to a large or important building

endure
[en door′, -dyoor′, in-]
v. 1. to tolerate; to suffer
2. to last; to continue

gateway
[gāt′ wā]
n. 1. a way to enter or gain access; an opening
2. a structure around an entrance that can be shut by a gate

panoramic
[pan′ ə ram′ ik]
adj. relating to a wide view; extensive; scenic

rectify
[rek′ tə fī′]
v. to correct; to put right; to fix

revitalize
[rē vīt′ l īz′]
v. to renew; to invigorate; to refresh

urban
[ûr′ bən]
adj. 1. concerned with a city
2. typical of a city or city life

Words to Watch

Which words would you like to practice with a bit more? Pick 3–5 words to study, and list them below. Write the word and its definition, and compose your own sentence using the word correctly. This extra practice could be the final touch to learning a word.

Word	Definition	Your Sentence
1. _____	_____	_____
_____	_____	_____
2. _____	_____	_____
_____	_____	_____
3. _____	_____	_____
_____	_____	_____
4. _____	_____	_____
_____	_____	_____
5. _____	_____	_____
_____	_____	_____

Chapter 22

Psychology

FAQs on Growing Up

Welcome to Kids Grow!

We hope you will enjoy interacting with parents, grandparents, guardians, educators, and others interested in the well-being of children. To help you become acquainted with the site, take a look at our Frequently Asked Questions (FAQs).

Q. What changes should I be aware of in my child's first five years?

5 A. Children go through numerous mental, emotional, and physical changes. Parents can help children to mature in a healthy fashion by understanding the **transformations** their children will experience. Two basic changes are the assertion of independence and an awareness of a wider world. Children begin establishing their independence from roughly ages one to three. This time is
10 commonly known as "The Terrible Twos," and it can be a trying period for adults when children routinely use "No" to assert themselves. From approximately ages three to six, children come to be aware of a wider world around them and start to ask "Why" (another test of the patience of nearby adults). Most of the changes will be **subtle**, with parents noticing differences over a
15 period of months. For more information on life stages, start by examining the pioneering studies done by psychologists Jean Piaget and Erik Erikson.

Q. Is there really a best parenting style?

A. The actions of parents can encourage or **suppress** a child's development. Three basic parenting styles exist: authoritarian, permissive, and authoritative.
20 Authoritarian parents set strict rules and punish children who don't obey, often by using physical methods. Children of parents who use this style often display **inhibitions**, such as being withdrawn. Conversely, permissive parents **defer** to their children's wishes, make few rules, and rarely follow through on those they do make. Children raised in this manner often display immature behavior and
25 have poor grades. As they grow, they may end up with drinking problems or participating in criminal activities. Between these two styles are authoritative parents who set high but realistic expectations for their children. They are also willing to talk to their children about the reasons for the rules they make. Authoritative parents tend to **endow** their children with the socially desirable
30 skills of self-reliance and high self-esteem.

Q. What help should I try to get for my teenager who is exhibiting possible psychological problems?

A. Start by looking for a therapist that you and your child feel comfortable talking with and who acts in a professional manner. Psychological problems may stem from biological and/or environmental factors. What happens in a child's early years is often crucial to one's later life. Many fears can be traced back to
35 **traumatic** childhood experiences, such as **claustrophobia** coming from being locked in a closet as a form of punishment. Various types of **obsessions**—cleanliness or aggression—may require therapy to overcome. Look for help from a professional who can find the **underlying** causes of a mental problem.

Predicting

For each set, write the definition on the line next to the word to which it belongs. If you are unsure, return to the reading, and underline any context clues you find. After you've made your predictions, check your answers against the Word List at the end of the chapter. Place a checkmark in the box next to each word whose definition you missed. These are the words you'll want to study closely.

Set One

to yield	restraints on behaviors	changes	to repress	hard to see

❑ 1. **transformations** (line 7) _____

❑ 2. **subtle** (line 14) _____

❑ 3. **suppress** (line 18) _____

❑ 4. **inhibitions** (line 22) _____

❑ 5. **defer** (line 22) _____

Set Two

disturbing	to furnish	original	a fear of small or enclosed places
ideas that excessively occupy the mind			

❑ 6. **endow** (line 29) _____

❑ 7. **traumatic** (line 35) _____

❑ 8. **claustrophobia** (line 35) _____

❑ 9. **obsessions** (line 36) _____

❑ 10. **underlying** (line 37) _____

Self-Tests

MyReadingLab Visit Chapter 22: Psychology in MyReadingLab to complete the Self-Test activities.

1 Match each vocabulary word with the words that could be associated with it.

Set One

_____ 1. suppress   a. change, makeover

_____ 2. traumatic   b. yield, delay

_____ 3. underlying   c. repress, conquer

_____ 4. defer   d. painful, shocking

_____ 5. transformation   e. basic, hidden

_____ 6. endow   f. slight, faint

_____ 7. subtle   g. constant, fixation

_____ 8. obsession   h. give, donate

_____ 9. inhibition   i. small, fear

_____ 10. claustrophobia   j. restraint, shyness

2 Finish the sentences with the vocabulary words. Use each word once.

VOCABULARY LIST

| obsession | underlying | defer | inhibition | endow |
| subtle | claustrophobia | traumatic | transformation | suppress |

1. This summer the core of the downtown area will experience an amazing _____ as five high-rises replace century-old structures.

2. The taste is _____, but I can detect a bit of cinnamon in these cookies.

3. Ms. Lee has promised to _____ two million dollars to the college when she dies.

4. Quan tried to _____ his feelings, but he eventually had to tell Araceli how he felt about her.

5. I will _____ to your judgment on this matter. You have much more experience in selecting wines.

6. Her _____ has prevented Hana from ever going in the water. She is afraid to wear a swimsuit and expose her body to public view.

7. Len won't be joining us on the submarine ride because he suffers from _____.

8. After thinking about it overnight, I was able to figure out the _____ meaning of the man's final words in the short story I just finished.

9. The woman's _____ with glass figurines has begun to have serious consequences. Her family can no longer eat at the dining room table because it is covered with them.

10. The automobile accident, which resulted in two fatalities, was a _____ experience for everyone involved.

3 Pretend you are engaged in the following activities, and match each to the word it suggests.

VOCABULARY LIST

| endow | subtle | defer | inhibition | suppress |
| traumatic | claustrophobia | underlying | transformation | obsession |

1. You are the head of a committee that decides to delay making an important decision until it receives a report that contains helpful information. _____

2. You are afraid to speak in front of more than four people. _____

3. You go from being inactive to running four times a week. _____

4. You discover that a fear of starving based on food shortages in your youth is the reason you overeat as an adult. _____

5. You give your children an interest in art by taking trips to museums. _____

6. You keep storing old newspapers in your garage even though you have no use for them. _____

7. You are editor of the school paper and decide not to run a story because it is unflattering to one of your friends. _____

8. You are afraid of getting into an elevator. _____

9. You suggest a vacation to your spouse by leaving brochures around the house. _____

10. You are four years old and separated from your parents in a busy mall. _____

Identify the two vocabulary words represented in the photographs.

1. _____

2. _____

Word Wise

Collocations

After her divorce, Yvette underwent a *complete transformation*. I didn't recognize her since she lost sixty pounds, cut and colored her hair, and started wearing dresses. (Chapter 22)

Because combat can be a *traumatic experience* for many soldiers, counseling can be an effective way to help them transition back to their daily activities. (Chapter 22)

Some students do not know how to make *judicious use of* their time; therefore, they end up doing projects at the last minute. (Chapter 23)

Though we all agree that the process for submitting forms could be easier, Elena continues to *belabor the point* at every staff meeting. (Chapter 23)

Interesting Etymologies

Claustrophobia (Chapter 22) comes from the Latin *claustrum,* "a place shut in," which comes from *claudere,* "to close." With the addition of the Greek *phobos,* "fear," claustrophobia means "a fear of small or enclosed places." The word was first used in the *British Medical Journal* in 1879.

Obsession (Chapter 22) comes from the Latin *obsessio,* "to occupy." In the past, it referred to an evil spirit that was trying to take over or occupy a person. Today the meaning is not as supernatural; it is "an idea that excessively occupies the mind."

Interactive Exercise

List two examples of a time or place that could be associated with or connected to each word.
Example: *transformation*—In the novel *Dr. Jekyll and Mr. Hyde*; a garden in the spring

claustrophobia

1. _____

2. _____

defer

1. _____

2. _____

endow

1. _____

2. _____

inhibition

1. _____

2. _____

obsession

1. _____

2. _____

subtle

1. _____

2. _____

suppress

1. _____

2. _____

transformation

1. _____

2. _____

traumatic

1. _____

2. _____

underlying

1. _____

2. _____

HINT

Play Games with Words

To make reading and vocabulary fun, learn to enjoy using words in recreational contexts.

- Pick up the Sunday paper, and do the crossword puzzle.
- Buy popular games that are based on using words such as Scattergories, Bananagrams, Scrabble, or Boggle. Invite your friends over to play. Also try online games such as Words with Friends.
- Play simple word games when traveling—for example, using words that are at least five letters long, the first person says a word and the next person must say a word that begins with the last letter of the previous word: backward, doctor, rabbit, talking, girls, etc.
- Write cards, e-mails, or text messages that play with language—for example, write a thank-you note that uses several synonyms to express what a "great" time you had: wonderful, magnificent, fabulous, splendid. Your friends will enjoy getting your cards or messages.

Word List

claustrophobia
[klô′ strə fō′ bē ə]

n. a fear of small or enclosed places

defer
[di fûr′]

v. 1. to submit to the decision or opinion of someone else; to yield
2. to postpone or delay

endow
[en dou′]

v. 1. to furnish; to equip
2. to give money as a donation

inhibition
[in′ hi bish′ ən, in′ i-]

n. 1. restraint of a behavior or desire or the condition causing such restraint
2. the act of holding back or blocking

obsession
[əb sesh′ ən, ob-]

n. an idea that excessively occupies the mind; a fascination

subtle
[sut′ l]

adj. 1. not obvious; hard to see; slight
2. difficult to understand; clever

suppress
[sə pres′]

v. 1. to deliberately inhibit an impulse or action; to repress
2. to withhold from publication; to censor
3. to dominate; to conquer

transformation
[trans′ fər mā′ shən]

n. 1. the act of changing
2. something that has been changed

traumatic
[trə mat′ ik, trô-]

adj. 1. psychologically painful; shocking; disturbing
2. relating to or causing a wound

underlying
[un′ dər li′ ing]

adj. 1. basic; original
2. concealed but detectable

Words to Watch

Which words would you like to practice with a bit more? Pick 3–5 words to study, and list them below. Write the word and its definition, and compose your own sentence using the word correctly. This extra practice could be the final touch to learning a word.

Word	Definition	Your Sentence
1.		
2.		
3.		
4.		
5.		

Chapter 23

Career Development

Resume Building

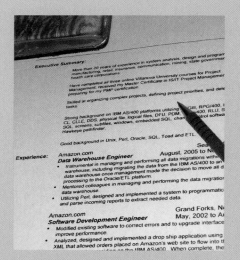

Finding a Job

A **resume** can help you get that important first interview. You want to make it **apparent** to the employer that you have the skills to be an excellent colleague. Even if you will not be looking for
5 a job right away, it is important to know the parts of a resume so you can begin compiling the necessary information to have it available when you are ready to job hunt. The following is an overview of the process for creating a resume.

10 First, decide whether to write a chronological or skill-based resume. Most people list their work history by time, but when you haven't worked much, it can be better to emphasize the skills you have that fit the job. If you make **judicious** use of
15 your time, you can draft a resume in little more than an hour. **Consolidate** your information into three basic groups: contact information, work history, and education.

In your contact information, include your name,
20 address, phone number(s), and e-mail address. In a **supplementary** section, you can add personal information such as organizations you belong to that relate to the job, as well as skills that show your aptitude for the position, such as foreign languages you speak. 25

Next list your previous jobs. Write the name of the company and city and state where it is located, the dates you started and ended working there, your job title, the duties you performed including equipment or technology you used, and skills the job required. Also 30 list promotions, awards, or other positive experiences involved with the job. Do the same for each of your past jobs. Add volunteer work if it is **pertinent** to the job. You usually don't need to go back more than ten years, but if you have significant information, go back 35 further.

Then list your education from high school on. Write the name of the school, the city and state where it is located, what degree or certificate you earned, courses that relate to your job objective, and 40 awards or other pertinent activities (such as being in student government or an officer in a club). Don't forget **seminars**, workshops, or other types of meetings as learning experiences.

Congratulations! You have just finished a basic 45 resume in a short time. Use a computer to organize the information. Your resume may have to **undergo** a few drafts as you make it easy to read, professional looking, and not more than two pages. Before you finish the resume, it is a good idea to **confer** with a 50 trusted friend for advice on how the resume looks and sounds. It is always helpful to get another opinion before sending out an important document. We won't **belabor** this point, but carefully proofread all of the information to make sure that it is correct 55 and that you haven't misspelled anything. If you are mailing your resume, make copies of it on quality paper. Many companies today, however, ask prospective employees to submit a resume online. No matter the method you use, if you have done a 60 good job of matching your skills to the company's needs, be prepared for follow-up phone calls!

Predicting

For each set, write the definition on the line next to the word to which it belongs. If you are unsure, return to the reading, and underline any context clues you find. After you've made your predictions, check your answers against the Word List at the end of the chapter. Place a checkmark in the box next to each word whose definition you missed. These are the words you'll want to study closely.

Set One

to combine	a brief document of skills and experiences	obvious
additional	wise	

❑ 1. **resume** (line 1) _____

❑ 2. **apparent** (line 2) _____

❑ 3. **judicious** (line 14) _____

❑ 4. **consolidate** (line 16) _____

❑ 5. **supplementary** (line 21) _____

Set Two

to experience	related	to overstress	to consult together	meetings

❑ 6. **pertinent** (line 33) _____

❑ 7. **seminars** (line 43) _____

❑ 8. **undergo** (line 47) _____

❑ 9. **confer** (line 50) _____

❑ 10. **belabor** (line 54) _____

Self-Tests

MyReadingLab Visit Chapter 23: Career Development in MyReadingLab to complete the Self-Test activities.

1 In each group, circle the word that does not have a connection to the other three words.

1. apparent	obvious	unclear	evident
2. class	seminar	meeting	party
3. extra	main	additional	supplementary
4. resume	summary	novel	work history
5. wise	stupid	judicious	thoughtful
6. belabor	overstress	beat	ignore
7. pertinent	related	unimportant	significant
8. bestow	confer	retreat	consult
9. avoid	experience	suffer	undergo
10. strengthen	consolidate	divide	unite

2 Use the vocabulary words to complete the resumes below. Use each word once.

VOCABULARY LIST

conferred   pertinent   consolidated   supplementary   seminars

Resume One

Technolife, Office Manager   San Jose, California   June 2002–March 2015

Main Duties: I oversaw 30 employees, gathered (1)_____ information to write annual

personnel reviews, and (2)_____ reports from five departments into a monthly summary.

I also regularly (3)_____ with upper management as well as engineers and developers to

keep the office running smoothly. (4)_____ Duties: I periodically organized company

(5)_____ on efficiency methods and successful ways to work with others.

VOCABULARY LIST

belabor   undergone   judicious   apparent   resumes

Resume Two

Bachelor's Degree in History, Minor in Business   Earl College, McAllen, Texas   May 2015

Pertinent courses: Business History examined changes American companies have (6)_____

in the last three hundred years; Money and Power explored trends that are readily (7)_____

in today's marketplace and practices that are not as evident. My senior seminar paper "A Point to

(8)_____: A Historical Look at Solving Business Conflicts" was awarded Best History

Composition of the Year.

   Accomplishments: Through (9)_____ use of my time, I earned a 3.8 grade

point average, worked 25 hours a week in the Career Center tutoring students on how to write

(10)_____, and played in the marching band.

Identify the two vocabulary words represented in the drawings.

Word Visions

1. _____

2. _____

3 Complete the sentences using the vocabulary words. Use each word once.

VOCABULARY LIST

confer	undergo	apparent	resume	consolidated
pertinent	seminar	belabored	judicious	supplementary

---

1. The _____ on financial planning helped me decide what to do with the money I inherited from my aunt.

2. The lecture last week proved to be extremely _____ to today's test. Half of the questions on the test were from the information in that lecture.

3. Reading the _____ materials will help you to better understand the ideas in this course.

4. It is _____ that Akira didn't finish the book; otherwise, he would certainly have mentioned the death of the hero in his report.

5. After all of your hard work, the college is proud to _____ upon you the degree of Bachelor of Science.

6. On Saturday, I will _____ surgery to fix my knee problem from an old football injury.

7. My son felt I _____ the point, but I wanted to stress that 10:00 p.m. was the latest he could stay out.

8. The hiring committee was impressed with his _____. He had every skill needed for the job.

9. The corporation _____ its position as the major grocery retailer in the area by opening six more stores this year.

10. Thanks to the _____ use of club funds throughout the year, we have enough money left for a New Year's party.

Word Wise

Internet Activity: Find an Image

You have been working with visuals throughout this text. Now it is your turn to find visuals for some of the vocabulary words. Start by looking up these words at Google Images:

longevity (Chapter 20)   transformation (Chapter 22)

revitalize (Chapter 21)   seminar (Chapter 23)

Did seeing images of the words help you to better remember their meanings? Were any of the images surprising?

Next pick three vocabulary words from the text that excite your curiosity as to how they might be represented by a photograph or illustration. You can again use Google Images or another site you find on the Web. For one of the words, select an image that you think exemplifies the meaning of the word, and print it out. Be prepared to share the image in class. Write the three words you have selected below.

1. _____

2. _____

3. _____

Interactive Exercise

Finish the sentence starters. The first five include one of the vocabulary words in the starter. For the second five, use each of the following vocabulary words once in your completed sentences: apparent, confer, consolidate, pertinent, and undergo.

1. Supplementary activities or experiences I could list on a resume include _____
   _____

2. During a job interview, I would want to belabor the point that I am _____
   _____

3. Two schools I would list on my resume are _____
   _____

4. I would be interested in attending a seminar on _____

5. I make judicious use of my time by _____

6. As a child I thought, _____
   _____

7. I would like a job where _____
   _____

8. If I were applying for a job overseas, I would _____
   _____

9. If I had a problem at work, I could _____
   _____

10. To make my life easier, I should _____
    _____

Conversation Starters

An excellent way to review the vocabulary words and help to make them your own is to use them when you are speaking. Gather three to five friends or classmates, and use one or more of the conversation starters below. Before you begin talking, have each person write down six of the vocabulary words he or she will use during the conversation. Share your lists with each other to check that you did not all pick the same six words. Try to cover all of the words you want to study, whether you are reviewing one, two, or more chapters.

1. What foods do you eat regularly that are especially nutritious? What foods should you eat less of because they aren't very nutritious?
2. Would you like to live in the urban environment described in the Chapter 21 reading? Why do you feel this way?
3. What makes raising children a pleasure? What makes it a challenge?
4. Of the three basic groups that resume information should be consolidated into, which would be the hardest part for you to put together? Why would this section be challenging?

Word List

apparent
[ə par′ ənt, ə pâr′-]
 adj. plain; obvious; open to view

belabor
[bi lā′ bər]
 v. to overstress; to explain or work at excessively; to beat

confer
[kən fûr′]
 v. 1. to consult together; to compare views
  2. to bestow, such as a degree or honor

consolidate
[kən sol′ i dāt′]
 v. 1. to combine; to unite; to make more compact
  2. to make secure or firm; to strengthen

judicious
[jo͞o dish′ əs]
 adj. wise; having good judgment; careful

pertinent
[pûr′ tin ənt]
 adj. related; important; to the point

resume, résumé, or resumé
[rez′ oo mā′, rez′ oo mā′]
 n. a brief document of skills and experiences prepared by a job applicant; a summary

seminar
[sem′ ə när′]
 n. a meeting or class for discussion of a specific subject

supplementary
[sə′ plə men′ tə rē, -men′ trē]
 adj. additional; extra; accompanying

undergo
[un′ dər gō′]
 v. 1. to experience; to feel
  2. to endure; to suffer

Words to Watch

Which words would you like to practice with a bit more? Pick 3–5 words to study, and list them below. Write the word and its definition, and compose your own sentence using the word correctly. This extra practice could be the final touch to learning a word.

	Word	Definition	Your Sentence
1.	_____	_____	_____
	_____	_____	_____
2.	_____	_____	_____
	_____	_____	_____
3.	_____	_____	_____
	_____	_____	_____
4.	_____	_____	_____
	_____	_____	_____
5.	_____	_____	_____
	_____	_____	_____

Chapter 24

Review

Focus on Chapters 20–23

The following activities give you the opportunity to further interact with the vocabulary words you've been learning. By taking tests, answering questions, using visuals, doing a crossword puzzle, and working with others, you will see which words you know well and which ones need additional study.

Self-Tests   MyReadingLab   Visit Chapter 24: Review in MyReadingLab to complete the Self-Test activities.

LO 4,8   **1** Match each term with its synonym in Set One and its antonym in Set Two.

Synonyms

Set One

_____	1. rectify	a. related
_____	2. pertinent	b. correct
_____	3. obsession	c. discuss
_____	4. complement	d. fascination
_____	5. confer	e. balance

Antonyms

Set Two

_____	6. deficiency	f. deteriorate
_____	7. defer	g. split
_____	8. underlying	h. advance
_____	9. revitalize	i. obvious
_____	10. consolidate	j. excess

Remember to add words to Word Reactions on page 175 after completing the Review chapter activities.

LO 1 **2** Pick the word that best completes each sentence.

1. The bank was such an impressive _____ that people felt confident leaving their money there.

   a. obsession   b. antidote   c. deficiency   d. edifice

2. I am working with a therapist to conquer my shyness. It is a(n) _____ that keeps me at home at nights when I would like to be out meeting new people.

   a. anemia   b. inhibition   c. urban   d. claustrophobia

3. The club president decided the meeting would _____ at 6 a.m.; I hope I can get everyone to come that early.

   a. convene   b. complement   c. endure   d. consolidate

4. It was easy to write a _____ once I got started, and organizing the information about my past jobs and education helped me think about what I want to do with my future.

   a. resume   b. gateway   c. seminar   d. transformation

5. This job was supposed to be a _____ to a more exciting position in the company, but I have been stuck here for three years.

   a. longevity   b. seminar   c. transformation   d. gateway

6. There are only a _____ number of hours in the day, so it is important that people learn how to effectively use all of them.

   a. panoramic   b. pertinent   c. finite   d. subtle

7. I feel it is essential to _____ with every family member about important choices in our lives. Everyone has a valuable viewpoint to bring to the decision-making process.

   a. rectify   b. confer   c. defer   d. undergo

8. The _____ on easy ways to create better eating habits will provide information that students can start using right away.

   a. obsession   b. edifice   c. seminar   d. complement

LO 1 **3** Pick the vocabulary word that best completes the sentence. Use each word once.

definitive	eclectic	underlying	subtle	supplementary

1. The music was _____. It softly played in the background, giving the restaurant a romantic air, but it wasn't so loud that we couldn't easily hold a quiet conversation.

2. The _____ display of time periods at Bev's house is amazing. She has furnishings from every decade in the twentieth century.

3. I had to go to the library to check out the _____ materials my instructor had put on reserve. The books weren't required, but she said they would be helpful to look over.

4. I consider *Grill the Right Way* the _____ source when I have a question about barbequing.

5. It's true that Yoshito made a few mistakes at work today, but someone needs to talk with him to learn the _____ reason as to why he is so upset.

4 Complete the following sentences that illustrate collocations. The rest of the collocation is in italics. Use each word or phrase once.

| the point | experience | reached a | plan | use of | in | complete |

1. Going shoe shopping with my sister was a *traumatic* _____. After we spent six hours at three stores, she bought only one pair of shoes.

2. Now that I am working two jobs and going to college, I have learned how to make *judicious* _____ my time.

3. The committee _____ *consensus* on how to spend the money after three hours of intense discussion.

4. A nutritionist has helped me to develop a *comprehensive* _____ to lose weight.

5. We drove by our old house, and the new owners have given it a _____ *transformation*. They added a second story, built a porch, and put in a huge flower garden out front.

6. The doctor said I could be suffering from a *deficiency* _____ an essential vitamin or mineral, so he recommended I get a blood test done.

7. My mother said she would not *belabor* _____ that I should call more often, but then over the next two weeks she e-mailed and texted me reminders to call her.

5 Fill in the missing meaning for the underlined word part.

| against | limit | give | everywhere | close | best | condition | fill |

1. I enjoy climbing the hill near my house in the evening because it gives me a <u>pan</u>oramic view of the town below. I can see _____ I traveled during the day.

2. One of the best gifts parents can _____ to a child is a love of reading. Fortunately, my parents en<u>dow</u>ed a fondness for books by taking me to the library since I was three.

3. My husband finally acknowledged that there is <u>fin</u>ite room in the garage. He promises that he will _____ his purchases of new tools so that he actually has space to work in there.

4. When I was little, my mom said she had an <u>ant</u>idote for boredom: She handed me a book. Since then I have found that books fight _____ every type of boredom.

5. Min usually takes a sup<u>ple</u>mentary job during the winter to _____ in for a shortage of income at that time of year.

6. I suffer from <u>claustro</u>phobia, so I don't like to _____ the door to my bedroom. The room is small, and I feel confined with the door shut.

7. By discovering your <u>opt</u>imum study time, you will be at your _____ to process new information.

8. Because Mariana is often tired, she might be suffering from some type of _____, such as anem<u>ia</u>.

6 Finish the story using the vocabulary words below. Use each word once.

VOCABULARY LIST

apparent	undergo	convene	domain	endure	pertinent
rectify	subtle	longevity	traumatic	optimum	suppressing

Just Relax

For over a year, I had been suffering from various aches and pains, but several doctors couldn't find an exact cause. The pain I sometimes had to (1)_____ was unbearable. I was ready to (2)_____ any type of surgery or procedure available to feel better. My friend then told me about a spa that uses nontraditional healing methods. She said that the (3)_____ of some of the clients there was simply amazing. She had heard that at least three dozen of them were over 110. I was ready to try anything to (4)_____ my problems, so that afternoon I went home and signed up for a week's stay.

When I arrived, I was surprised to find a beautiful courtyard filled with birds. The serene scene set the tone for my treatments. I felt like I was entering the (5)_____ of master healers. In my initial consultation with a doctor, she noted that I might be (6)_____ feelings that were bringing on my pains. She said we would (7)_____ in the aromatherapy room at 9 a.m. to begin my treatments.

After that first session, it was (8)_____ to me that the spa was going to help. I already felt a (9)_____ but definite relaxation in my entire body. In the afternoon, I joined a therapy session where we all shared (10)_____ experiences we had undergone at some point in our lives. People told about being in car accidents, losing a loved one, and falling off cliffs. At first I didn't see how this session was (11)_____ to my health, but I actually felt physically better after sharing. During my week stay, I enjoyed herbal wraps, massages, and acupuncture treatments. I continued to feel better and better after each session. I knew I wasn't quite at my (12)_____ health when I left, but I was much closer to it than I had been in years.

Interactive Exercise

Answer the following questions to further test your understanding of the vocabulary words.

1. What is something (a place, an item, a quality) you want to revitalize?

_____

2. What is there a deficiency of in your life? What could be a gateway to fixing this deficiency?

_____

_____

3. What are two hardships you have had to undergo?

_____

_____

4. What are two urges or actions you think people often try to suppress?

_____

_____

5. If you were to use an eclectic design in your house, what styles would you pick?

_____

6. Would you say you are judicious in your spending habits? Explain why you are or aren't.

_____

_____

7. What do you see as three possible benefits to urban living?

_____

_____

8. What are two things people commonly have obsessions about?

_____

_____

9. Where would you go in your area to enjoy a panoramic view?

_____

10. List three kinds of people (e.g., a friend) someone would confer with if he or she was having a problem.

_____

_____

11. If you and four of your friends were given half a million dollars to give away, where would you choose to endow the money? Would it be easy for the five of you to reach a consensus?

_____

_____

12. What is one of your antidotes for relieving sadness or disappointment?

_____

LO 6,7 **Story Forming**

Select either photograph, and write a short story (one to two paragraphs) using the picture as inspiration. You can let your imagination go with this exercise. Use at least six of the vocabulary words below in the story. Feel free to add word endings (i.e., -s, -ing, -ly) if needed. Share the story with your classmates—read your stories aloud or pass them around to read silently. Then discuss how the same picture produces different stories and different uses of the words.

VOCABULARY LIST

apparent	complement
domain	edifice
endure	endow
finite	inhibition
judicious	optimum
resume	revitalize
seminar	urban
underlying	transformation

Crossword Puzzle

LO 3

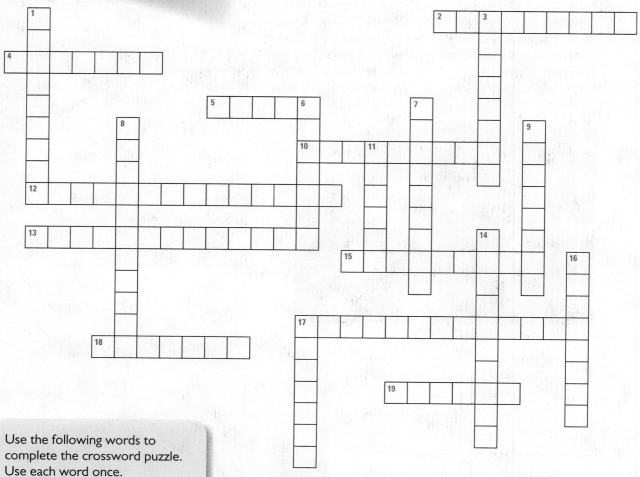

Use the following words to complete the crossword puzzle. Use each word once.

VOCABULARY LIST

anemia	eclectic
antidote	longevity
belabor	obsession
claustrophobia	panoramic
comprehensive	pertinent
consensus	rectify
consolidate	subtle
convene	supplementary
defer	suppress
definitive	undergo

Across

2. Howard Hughes had this about washing his hands.
4. to experience or to suffer
5. opposite of rush
10. "I'm glad we all agree."
12. fear of enclosed places
13. additional or accompanying
15. When writing a paper, you want to include only this type of information.
17. complete or full
18. to overstress
19. "I feel weak."

Down

1. for example, from a mountain-top or the roof of a high-rise building
3. This action can apply to a feeling, a newspaper article, or a group of people.
6. to correct
7. living to be 120, for example
8. putting three partially filled jars of pickles into one jar, for example
9. a cure
11. hard to see
14. opposite of unreliable
16. diverse
17. "I call this meeting to order."

Make Learning Fun

Think about the kinds of activities you like to do, and see if you can incorporate the traits involved in those activities into your learning experiences. If you like group activities (team sports, going to big parties), create study groups. If you like to draw, add visual elements to your notes, draw what happens in a story you read, or make a diagram to help you understand a concept. The more you enjoy what you do, whether in school or at work, the more you want to do it. Find the ways to make your life and learning fun.

Mix It Up LO 3,8

Drama

Get together with a few classmates to play charades. Use the words below or any of the vocabulary words you want to study. You can write the words on slips of paper and pick them out of a bowl or use your flash cards. One person picks a word, and the other people try to guess what word the person is acting out. You cannot use any words or sounds as you act out the word.

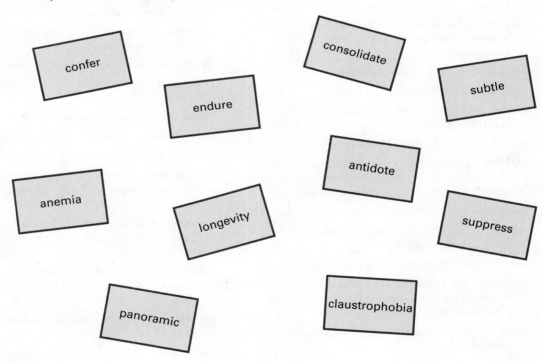

confer

consolidate

endure

subtle

anemia

antidote

longevity

suppress

panoramic

claustrophobia

Glossary

A

abhor   *v.* to detest; to loathe; to hate

acclimate   *v.* to get used to a new setting or situation; to adapt; to adjust

acronym   *n.* a word or abbreviation formed from the initial letters or groups of letters of the words in a name or phrase

adage   *n.* a traditional saying; a proverb

adhere   *v.* 1. to follow closely, such as a plan; to support something   2. to stick together; to hold

advocate   *n.* a person who supports a cause   *v.* to support or urge; to recommend

alibi   *n.* an excuse or explanation, especially used to avoid blame

amendment   *n.* 1. the formal alteration of a document; revision   2. the act of changing for the better; improvement

amiable   *adj.* good-natured; agreeable

amorous   *adj.* being in love; passionate

anemia   *n.* a lack of oxygen-carrying material in the blood, which results in weakness

annihilate   *v.* to destroy; to defeat completely

antidote   *n.* 1. something that prevents an unwanted effect; a cure   2. a medicine or other remedy for counteracting the effects of a poison or a disease

antipathy   *n.* an aversion; an opposition in feeling; dislike

apathy   *n.* lack of interest; absence or suppression of emotion or excitement

apparent   *adj.* plain; obvious; open to view

arbitrary   *adj.* 1. determined by chance or impulse, not by need or reason; random   2. based on individual judgment or preference

assent   *v.* to agree or concur   *n.* agreement, as to a proposal

asset   *n.* an advantage; a desirable thing or quality

assurance   *n.* 1. self-confidence; certainty   2. a guarantee; a pledge or promise

aversion   *n.* 1. a strong dislike of something and a desire to avoid it; hatred   2. a cause or object of such a dislike

avert   *v.* 1. to prevent   2. to turn away or aside

B

belabor   *v.* to overstress; to explain or work at excessively; to beat

berate   *v.* to scold harshly; to criticize

bewilder   *v.* to confuse, baffle, or puzzle

bias   *n.* a preference or prejudice that can hinder impartial decision making; unfairness   *v.* to influence, usually in an unfair manner

C

capacity   *n.* 1. the ability to do or make something; capability   2. the ability to hold something   3. the position in which a person functions; role

cease   *v.* to put an end to; to stop; to discontinue

charisma   *n.* a special quality of leadership that inspires devotion; charm; allure

circumspection   *n.* watchfulness; caution; care

circumvent   *v.* 1. to go around   2. to avoid by cleverness; to elude

clandestine   *adj.* secret; private

claustrophobia   *n.* a fear of small or enclosed places

cliché   *n.* a commonplace or overused expression or idea

colloquialism   *n.* an expression used in conversational or informal language, not usually appropriate for formal writing

commitment   *n.* 1. a pledge to do something; a promise   2. the state of being devoted to a belief, a person, or course of action; loyalty

complement   *v.* to serve as a completion to; to balance or complete   *n.* something that completes or makes up a whole

comprehensive   *adj.* large in content or reach; complete; full

compromise   *v.* 1. to arrive at a settlement by yielding on certain points; to cooperate; to bargain   2. to lower or weaken, such as standards   *n.* a settlement of differences where each side yields on certain points; a deal

concise   *adj.* expressing much in a few words; brief

condone   *v.* 1. to forgive or pardon; to excuse   2. to overlook; to ignore something illegal or offensive; to give unstated approval to

confer   *v.* 1. to consult together; to compare views   2. to bestow, such as a degree or honor

consensus   *n.* a unity of opinion; agreement; harmony

conservationist   *n.* a person who works to save the environment; an environmentalist

consolidate   *v.* 1. to combine; to unite; to make more compact   2. to make secure or firm; to strengthen

convene   *v.* 1. to assemble, usually for a public purpose; to organize   2. to summon to appear

covert   *adj.* concealed; secret; disguised

credibility   *n.* trustworthiness; believability

cursory   *adj.* going rapidly over something, without noticing details; hasty; superficial

D

decipher   *v.* to decode; to make out; to make sense of

decisive   *adj.* 1. displaying firmness; determined; sure   2. crucial; important

defer   *v.* 1. to submit to the decision or opinion of someone else; to yield   2. to postpone or delay

deficiency   *n.* a lack or shortage

definitive   *adj.* most reliable or complete; final

defraud   *v.* to take away a right, money, or property by deception; to cheat

delude   *v.* to mislead; to deceive; to fool

dependable   *adj.* trustworthy; responsible

dissent   *v.* to differ in feeling or opinion, especially from the majority   *n.* a difference of opinion

domain   *n.* 1. a territory of control; a kingdom   2. an area of concern; a field

E

eclectic   *adj.* selecting from various sources; diverse

edifice   *n.* a building or a structure, usually used when referring to a large or important building

elicit   *v.* to draw or bring out; to obtain

embellish   *v.* 1. to exaggerate; to elaborate; to add details   2. to decorate

emissary   *n.* 1. a representative sent on a mission; a delegate   2. an agent sent on a secret mission

enable   *v.* to make possible; to permit

encroachment   *n.* the act of gradually taking over an area or possessions that belong to someone else; an intrusion

endemic   *adj.* natural to a particular area; native

endow   *v.* 1. to furnish; to equip   2. to give money as a donation

endure   *v.* 1. to tolerate; to suffer   2. to last; to continue

euphemism   *n.* a mild or vague expression substituted for one considered harsh

euphoria   *n.* a feeling of extreme well-being or extreme happiness

exemplify   *v.* to show by example; to model; to represent

F

facilitate   *v.* to make easier; to assist

figurehead   *n.* a person in a position of leadership who has no real power

finite   *adj.* 1. having boundaries; limited   2. existing for a limited time; temporary

frenzied   *adj.* wild; agitated; mad

G

gateway   *n.* 1. a way to enter or gain access; an opening   2. a structure around an entrance that can be shut by a gate

glitch   *n.* a minor malfunction or technical error

H

habitat   *n.* 1. the environment where a plant or animal typically lives; surroundings   2. the place where something or someone is usually found

homonym   *n.* one of two or more words that have the same sound and sometimes the same spelling but differ in meaning

I

impede   *v.* to block; to hinder

impending   *adj.* 1. about to happen; approaching   2. threatening; looming

implement   *v.* to apply; to put into practice   *n.* a tool or utensil

imply   *v.* to state indirectly; to suggest; to hint

impose   *v.* to force on others

incredulous   *adj.* skeptical; doubtful; disbelieving

indicate   *v.* 1. to be a sign of; to show the need for; to reveal   2. to point out or point to

infrastructure   *n.* 1. foundations countries depend on, such as roads and power plants   2. the basic features of an organization

inhibition   *n.* 1. restraint of a behavior or desire or the condition causing such restraint   2. the act of holding back or blocking

innate   *adj.* 1. possessed at birth; natural   2. possessed as an essential trait

intermittent   *adj.* stopping and beginning again; periodic; irregular

intrigue   *v.* to fascinate   *n.* a scheme; a plot

invoke   *v.* 1. to cite or use for support   2. to call on for support or inspiration; to summon

irony   *n.* 1. a clash between what is expected to happen and what really does, often used humorously in literature   2. the use of words to state the opposite of their precise meaning

J

jovial   *adj.* merry; good-humored; cheerful

judicious   *adj.* wise; having good judgment; careful

justify   *v.* to show or prove to be right or fair; to defend

L

lax   *adj.* not strict; careless; loose

liability   *n.* a disadvantage; an undesirable thing or quality

longevity   *n.* long life; length of life or service

M

mammal   *n.* warm-blooded vertebrate (animal with a backbone)

miscalculation   *n.* a mistake in planning or forecasting

misgiving   *n.* a feeling of doubt or distrust

moratorium   *n.* suspension of an activity; an end or halt

N

notion   *n.* 1. an idea, belief, or opinion   2. an impulse or urge

nurture   *v.* to encourage; to educate or train   *n.* the act of promoting growth; rearing

O

oblivious   *adj.* unaware; forgetful

obsession   *n.* an idea that excessively occupies the mind; a fascination

omnipotent   *adj.* having great or unlimited authority or power

omnipresent   *adj.* present everywhere at once

omnivorous   *adj.* eating all types of foods

optimist   *n.* a person who looks on the bright side; one who expects a positive result

optimum   *adj.* most favorable; best   *n.* the best condition or amount for a specific situation

ordeal   *n.* a harsh or trying test or experience

ovation   *n.* applause; approval

P

pandemonium   *n.* disorder; chaos

panoramic   *adj.* relating to a wide view; extensive; scenic

pertinent   *adj.* related; important; to the point

phishing   *n.* the practice of luring innocent Internet users to a fake Web site by using real-looking e-mail with the goal to steal personal information or introduce a virus

potential   *n.* the ability for growth or development   *adj.* possible but not yet realized

precise   *adj.* 1. exact; accurate; definite   2. strictly correct; demanding

presentiment   *n.* a feeling that something is about to happen, especially something bad; foreboding; expectation

proliferate   *v.* to increase in number; to spread rapidly; to grow

propensity   *n.* a tendency; a leaning; a preference

protocol   *n.* 1. a code of correct behavior; the etiquette diplomats follow   2. a plan for a medical treatment or scientific experiment

provocative   *adj.* stimulating; exciting; troubling

R

rectify   *v.* to correct; to put right; to fix

recuperate   *v.* 1. to return to health or regain strength; to recover   2. to recover from a financial loss

resourceful   *adj.* able to deal skillfully with new situations; capable; inventive

restrain   *v.* to hold back or control; to prevent from doing something

resume, résumé, or resumé   *n.* a brief document of skills and experiences prepared by a job applicant; a summary

revitalize   *v.* to renew; to invigorate; to refresh

S

scrutinize   *v.* to examine carefully, especially looking for errors; to inspect

seclusion   *n.* solitude; a sheltered or isolated place

seminar   *n.* a meeting or class for discussion of a specific subject

serenity   *n.* peacefulness; tranquility

spam   *n.* junk e-mail, often advertising, sent to multiple individuals   *v.* 1. to send unwanted e-mail   2. to send to multiple individuals   *n.* (capital S) a canned meat product made mainly from pork

subjugate   *v.* to conquer; to master; to dominate

submissive   *adj.* obedient; passive

subtle   *adj.* 1. not obvious; hard to see; slight   2. difficult to understand; clever

supplementary   *adj.* additional; extra; accompanying

suppress   *v.* 1. to deliberately inhibit an impulse or action; to repress   2. to withhold from publication; to censor   3. to dominate; to conquer

surpass   *v.* to go beyond; to excel; to be superior to

susceptible   *adj.* open to an influence; sensitive

synopsis   *n.* a brief statement that gives a general idea; a summary

T

terminology   *n.* the words belonging to a specialized subject; the study of terms for particular subjects; vocabulary

transformation   *n.* 1. the act of changing   2. something that has been changed

transitory   *adj.* not lasting; temporary

traumatic   *adj.* 1. psychologically painful; shocking; disturbing   2. relating to or causing a wound

U

undergo   *v.* 1. to experience; to feel   2. to endure; to suffer

underlying   *adj.* 1. basic; original   2. concealed but detectable

undermine   *v.* 1. to weaken or damage (such as health or morale) by small stages   2. to weaken or cause to collapse by removing basic supports

urban   *adj.* 1. concerned with a city   2. typical of a city or city life

V

validity   *n.* 1. authenticity; legal soundness   2. strength; authority

venture   *v.* to brave; to take the risk of   *n.* an undertaking involving risk; a business project

virile   *adj.* masculine; manly; strong

virtual   *adj.* 1. created or run by a computer; simulated   2. almost existing; near

Z

zealous   *adj.* enthusiastic; eager; passionate

zenith   *n.* the highest point; the peak; the top

zoology   *n.* the study of animals, including their behavior and development

Create Your Own Flash Cards

Using flash cards can be an immensely helpful way to study vocabulary words. The process of making the flash cards will aid you in remembering the meanings of the words. Index cards work well as flash cards, or photocopy the following flash card template to get started. Put the word and the pronunciation on the front of the card. Elements you may want to include on the back of the card will vary according to the word and your preferred learning style. Consider the ideas below and find what works best for you.

1. **The part of speech:** Write an abbreviation for the part of speech, such as *n.* for noun or *v.* for verb. This addition will help when you are writing sentences.
2. **A simple definition:** Use the definitions in the book or modify them to something that has meaning for you. Use a definition you can remember.
3. **A sentence:** Make up your own sentence that correctly uses the word. Try to use a context clue to help you remember the word. It might help to put yourself or friends in the sentences to personalize your use of the word. If you really like a sentence from the book, you can use that too.
4. **A drawing:** If you are a visual learner, try drawing the word. Some words especially lend themselves to this method. Your drawing doesn't have to be fancy; it should just help you remember the meaning of the word.
5. **A mnemonic [ni mon′ ik] device:** These are methods to help your memory. They can be rhymes, formulas, or clues. For example: Station*e*ry with an *e* is the kind that goes in an *e*nvelope. Make up any connections you can between the word and its meaning.
6. **Highlight word parts:** Circle one or more word parts (prefixes, roots, or suffixes) that appear in the word and write the meaning(s) next to the word part: for example, fin̲ale. See the Word Parts chapters in the text for more on word parts.
    └→end

Whatever you do, make the cards personally meaningful. Find the techniques that work for you, and use them in creating your cards. Then make the time to study the cards. Carry them with you, and study them any chance you get. Also, find someone who will be tough in quizzing you with the cards. Have the person hold up a card, and you give the meaning and use the word in a sentence. Don't quit until you are confident that you know what each word means.

Sample card

Front

surpass

[sər pas′]

Back

v. to go beyond; to excel   I did it!

I surpassed my expectations
when I climbed the mountain.

Make Your Own Word Maps

Making a word map is a great way to visualize the meaning, synonym, and antonym for a word. By creating the map, you become more familiar with different aspects of the word. You can find the synonyms and antonyms in a dictionary or thesaurus, in some of the Word Lists or Self-Tests in this text, or come up with your own. To test yourself using a word map, cover one or more of the circles around the vocabulary word; then state the information in the covered circle(s). Another method is to cover the vocabulary word to see if you can identify the word using the meaning, synonym, and antonym. You can also ask a friend or classmate to cover up the information and quiz you on the word maps.

For some words, you may want to use one (or more) of the options below if it will help you better understand and remember the meaning of the word:

1. Write more than one synonym or antonym.
2. Put the part of speech under the vocabulary word.
3. Use different colors to outline or fill in the circles.
4. Add a circle with an example that applies to the word, such as who would do or use it.

To get started, photocopy the templates in this text or use a blank sheet of paper to make your word maps. Examples that illustrate the options using an adjective, verb, and noun follow.

Synonym: left circle

Vocabulary word: center circle

Antonym: right circle

Meaning: bottom circle

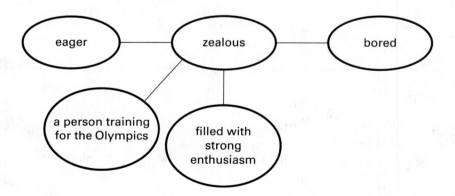

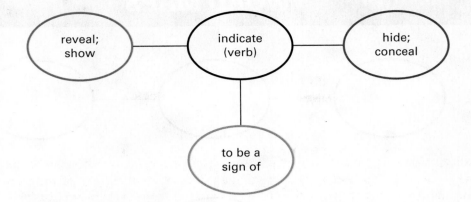

Note: For some nouns it may be tricky to find an antonym. If it becomes too difficult to find or think of one, don't stress about it.

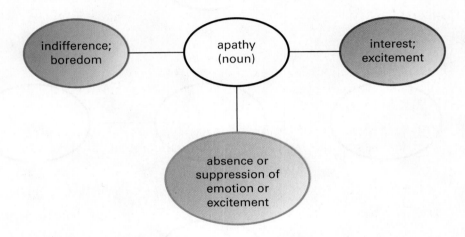

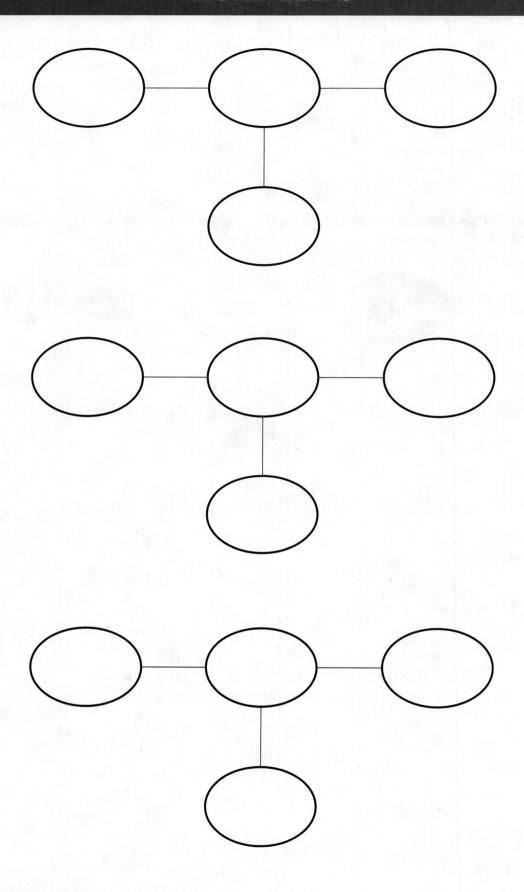

Use the following spaces to list your reactions to the vocabulary words in this text. Creating the lists will help you become more connected to the words by thinking closely about the words and their meanings. The activity will also make you more aware of your reactions to words in general. Return to this page after every Review chapter to add words to the lists (try to add at least six words each time). Continue a list on the back of this page if you need more space for any category.

Words I especially like

1. _____
2. _____
3. _____
4. _____
5. _____
6. _____
7. _____
8. _____
9. _____
10. _____

Very useful words

(see or use regularly)

1. _____
2. _____
3. _____
4. _____
5. _____
6. _____
7. _____
8. _____
9. _____
10. _____

Hard-to-pronounce words

1. _____
2. _____
3. _____
4. _____
5. _____
6. _____
7. _____
8. _____
9. _____
10. _____

Challenging-to-use words

1. _____
2. _____
3. _____
4. _____
5. _____
6. _____
7. _____
8. _____
9. _____
10. _____

Create a category

(e.g., funny, relates to my major)

_____

_____

_____

1. _____
2. _____
3. _____
4. _____
5. _____
6. _____
7. _____
8. _____
9. _____
10. _____

P

pandemonium, 53
panoramic, 145
pertinent, 157
phishing, 93
potential, 81
precise, 47
presentiment, 59
proliferate, 125
propensity, 125
protocol, 27
provocative, 53

R

rectify, 145
recuperate, 125
resourceful, 27
restrain, 21
resume, 157
revitalize, 145

S

scrutinize, 113
seclusion, 53
seminar, 157
serenity, 21
spam, 93
subjugate, 47
submissive, 21
subtle, 151
supplementary, 157
suppress, 151
surpass, 81
susceptible, 81
synopsis, 113

T

terminology, 15
transformation, 151
transitory, 59
traumatic, 151

U

undergo, 157
underlying, 151
undermine, 15
urban, 145

V

validity, 93
venture, 125
virile, 53
virtual, 27

Z

zealous, 15
zenith, 119
zoology, 87

Word Parts
am-, 28
anti-, 94
-ary, 28
circum-, 94
-cis-, 28
-cla-, 28
-clo-, 28
-clu-, 28
-cred-, 60
-don-, 94

-dot-, 94
-dow-, 94
eu-, 28
-fer-, 94
-fin-, 28
-fy, 28
-hab-, 94
-hib-, 94
-ia, 94
-ify, 28
-ism, 60
-ist, 60
mis-, 60
-mis-, 28
-mit-, 28
-ology, 94
omni-, 28
-opt-, 60
pan-, 94
-pend-, 60
-pens-, 60
-ple-, 28
-sens-, 60
-sent-, 60
sub-, 60
sup-, 60
trans-, 60
-ven-, 94
-vent-, 94
-vers-, 60
-vert-, 60
-voc-, 94
-vok-, 94